中国地质大学(武汉)2021年研究生精品教材建设项目(YJC2021302)资助

CATTI 二级笔译实务

A GUIDE TO TRANSLATING PRACTICE OF CATTI LEVEL 2

高永刚　甘　露　吴锦文　编著

图书在版编目(CIP)数据

CATTI 二级笔译实务/高永刚,甘露,吴锦文编著.—武汉:中国地质大学出版社,2022.12
ISBN 978-7-5625-5465-3

Ⅰ.①C⋯ Ⅱ.①高⋯ ②甘⋯ ③吴⋯ Ⅲ.①英语-翻译-资格考试-自学参考资料
Ⅳ.①H315.9

中国版本图书馆 CIP 数据核字(2022)第 227495 号

CATTI 二级笔译实务	高永刚　甘　露　吴锦文　编著
责任编辑:龙昭月　　　选题策划:周　豪　龙昭月	责任校对:徐蕾蕾
出版发行:中国地质大学出版社(武汉市洪山区鲁磨路388号)	邮编:430074
电　　话:(027)67883511　　传　　真:(027)67883580	E-mail:cbb@cug.edu.cn
经　　销:全国新华书店	http://cugp.cug.edu.cn
开本:787 毫米×1 092 毫米　1/16	字数:244 千字　　印张:9.75
版次:2022 年 12 月第 1 版	印次:2022 年 12 月第 1 次印刷
印刷:武汉市籍缘印刷厂	
ISBN 978-7-5625-5465-3	定价:49.00 元

如有印装质量问题请与印刷厂联系调换

Preface 序

全国翻译专业资格(水平)考试(China Accreditation Test for Translators and Interpreters,CATTI)是一项面向全社会的职业资格考试。CATTI考试分笔译和口译两类,设有一级、二级、三级,对翻译能力有着不同的要求。自2003年12月开考以来,其证书认可度不断提升。CATTI选拔的翻译人才在展现文化自信、讲好中国故事、促进中国的国际合作等方面发挥着重要作用。

市面上针对CATTI考试的指定教材、辅导教材林林总总,各有千秋:有偏重翻译理论的,有偏重翻译实践的;绝大多数是讲授英汉翻译的,少之又少是讲授汉英翻译的。如何从令人眼花缭乱的各类教材中选取有针对性的备考资料,是广大考生最关心的。

笔者从事MTI(master of translation and interpreting,翻译硕士)基础笔译教学工作已有10余年,一直致力于翻译教学实践的系统梳理和简单操作。本教材围绕CATTI二级笔译实务,聚焦于专业译员培养,是多年课堂翻译教学的结晶。在课堂教学中,笔者无数次就笔译实务真题的文章和句子进行拆解、归纳、调整;同时,很多学生反馈的独到心得也进一步完善了笔者提出的翻译策略。希望本教材能为大家指明翻译之道,让同学们在应考中从容应对。

本教材突出一个"新"字,有三大亮点:

(1)提出新理念:独创性地提出"主干+定状"的翻译理念。翻译的难点在于修饰成分的形式多样性。本书从句子组成入手,先从宏观的角度把握句子主体,再将焦点放在修饰上,修饰严格来讲就是定语和状语。换句话说,在英译中时先找出主干和修饰,再运用不同的策略处理定语和状语;在中译英时,把中文转换成中文的英文句式,使主干和修饰一目了然。这样,一个理念即可统领英汉互译:英译中强调作修饰成分的定语与状语如何处理;中译英强调把修饰成分处理成定语和状语。

(2)重视新逻辑:强调重视和呈现句子翻译中所体现的逻辑关系。在翻译实践中,一般认为主干和修饰之间有一定的逻辑关系,这点毋庸置疑。本教材认为逻辑关系在某些句子中也存在于修饰成分的定语和状语之间、定语之间、状语之间,只有全面认识逻辑关系的存在,才能更好地进行翻译。

(3)结合新媒体:积极探索教材和新媒体的结合形式。本教材的技巧部分全部配备了相应的视频讲解,同时建立了公众号,创设了同学们在学习过程中与教材的互联通道,公众号将不断推出文章,以求答疑释惑。

本书的出版除了作者之外还有更多人的辛勤付出与劳动。感谢中国地质大学出版社的编辑周豪和龙昭月,他们在此书出版的过程中调度得当,保障有力。感谢宋梦雨、李皓倩两位研究生在教材资料、视频制作、公众号推广以及部分章节的撰写校对等方面作出的积极贡献。感谢中国地质大学(武汉)研究生院对本教材的资助。

翻译是一门浩瀚无垠的学科,本书仅为CATTI二级笔译实务的讲解,难免挂一漏万,还望广大读者和翻译界同仁批评指正,笔者将感谢不尽,谢谢大家。

若有需要联系笔者的地方,请直接访问本教材的公众号:AAE_AllAboutEnglish。

高永刚

2020 年 10 月 10 日

于武汉

Content 目录

0 导 论 …………………………… (1)
　0.1 主 干 ………………………… (1)
　0.2 定语与状语 …………………… (2)
　0.3 转 译 ………………………… (2)
　0.4 逻 辑 ………………………… (3)

基础知识篇

1 中英文的差异 …………………… (6)
　1.1 形式差异 ……………………… (6)
　1.2 表述差异 ……………………… (8)
2 中英文句子的主干及修饰 ……… (11)
　2.1 主 干 ………………………… (11)
　2.2 修饰语 ………………………… (13)
3 定 语 …………………………… (15)
　3.1 定语的类型 …………………… (15)
　3.2 定语的位置 …………………… (16)
　3.3 定语的功能 …………………… (16)
4 状 语 …………………………… (19)
　4.1 修饰性状语 …………………… (19)
　4.2 评注性状语 …………………… (19)
　4.3 连接性状语 …………………… (20)

英译中篇

5 定 语 …………………………… (22)
　5.1 前 置 ………………………… (22)
　5.2 后 置 ………………………… (22)
　5.3 句 首 ………………………… (23)
　5.4 合 并 ………………………… (23)
　5.5 转 译 ………………………… (24)
　5.6 语序调整 ……………………… (24)
6 状 语 …………………………… (26)
　6.1 顺 译 ………………………… (26)
　6.2 倒 译 ………………………… (26)
　6.3 转 译 ………………………… (27)
　6.4 省 译 ………………………… (27)
7 同位语和插入语 ………………… (28)
　7.1 同位语 ………………………… (28)
　7.2 插入语 ………………………… (29)
8 转 译 …………………………… (31)
　8.1 词类转换 ……………………… (31)
　8.2 句子成分转译 ………………… (33)
9 逻 辑 …………………………… (34)
　9.1 显性的衔接 …………………… (34)
　9.2 隐性的连贯 …………………… (36)
10 长 句 …………………………… (39)
　10.1 单独处理分译法 ……………… (39)
　10.2 意合综合法 …………………… (39)
　10.3 习惯顺逆法 …………………… (40)
11 词和表达的选择 ………………… (41)
　11.1 词 …………………………… (41)
　11.2 表 达 ………………………… (43)
12 被动语态 ………………………… (46)
　12.1 变主动 ……………………… (46)

12.2　换说法 …………………… (48)
- **13　增减** ………………………… (49)
　　13.1　动　词 …………………… (49)
　　13.2　范畴词 …………………… (50)
　　13.3　代词连词 ………………… (50)
- **14　数词** ………………………… (52)
　　14.1　倍数的翻译 ……………… (52)
　　14.2　数词的归化与异化 ……… (53)
- **15　专有名词** …………………… (54)
　　15.1　人名与地名 ……………… (54)
　　15.2　组织机构和活动名称 …… (54)
　　15.3　报纸书名 ………………… (55)
　　15.4　影视剧歌曲 ……………… (55)

中译英篇

- **16　中文句子的拆解** …………… (58)
　　16.1　并列结构 ………………… (58)
　　16.2　主从结构 ………………… (60)
- **17　定语** ………………………… (65)
　　17.1　前　置 …………………… (65)
　　17.2　后　置 …………………… (65)
- **18　连动** ………………………… (68)
　　18.1　并列连动 ………………… (68)
　　18.2　从属连动 ………………… (68)
　　18.3　链式联动 ………………… (69)
- **19　多层并列** …………………… (71)
　　19.1　厘清主干 ………………… (71)
　　19.2　注意选词 ………………… (72)
　　19.3　合理连接 ………………… (72)
　　19.4　灵活变换 ………………… (73)
- **20　句子的连接** ………………… (75)
　　20.1　词或短语 ………………… (75)
　　20.2　非谓语动词 ……………… (75)
　　20.3　从　句 …………………… (76)
- **21　转译** ………………………… (78)
　　21.1　动转名 …………………… (78)
　　21.2　动转形副 ………………… (79)
　　21.3　形转名 …………………… (79)
　　21.4　名转动 …………………… (80)
　　21.5　范畴词转译 ……………… (80)
- **22　增减** ………………………… (82)
　　22.1　语法增减 ………………… (82)
　　22.2　语意增减 ………………… (82)
　　22.3　语体增减 ………………… (83)
　　22.4　范畴词省译 ……………… (84)
- **23　无主句** ……………………… (85)
　　23.1　补主语 …………………… (85)
　　23.2　译被动 …………………… (85)
　　23.3　找主语 …………………… (85)
　　23.4　换句型 …………………… (86)
- **24　主动变被动** ………………… (87)
　　24.1　实质被动句 ……………… (87)
　　24.2　"是"字句 ………………… (87)
　　24.3　主语泛指句 ……………… (88)
　　24.4　正式委婉句 ……………… (88)
　　24.5　特殊无主句 ……………… (88)
- **25　重复** ………………………… (89)
　　25.1　显性重复 ………………… (89)
　　25.2　隐性重复 ………………… (89)
- **26　四字结构** …………………… (91)
　　26.1　直　译 …………………… (91)
　　26.2　意　译 …………………… (91)
　　26.3　省　译 …………………… (92)
- **27　隐喻** ………………………… (93)
　　27.1　直　译 …………………… (93)
　　27.2　归　化 …………………… (93)
　　27.3　异　化 …………………… (94)
　　27.4　转换(转明喻) …………… (94)
　　27.5　释　义 …………………… (95)
- **28　特殊句式** …………………… (96)
　　28.1　处置"把" ………………… (96)
　　28.2　把……作为 ……………… (96)
　　28.3　祈使"把" ………………… (97)
　　28.4　双宾"把" ………………… (97)

28.5 致使"把" ……………………（97）

结论篇

29 "主干定状说"的本质 …………（100）
   29.1 英译中 ……………………（100）
   29.2 中译英 ……………………（100）

经典实战真题讲解篇

30 2017 年 5 月二级笔译实务真题 ………………………………（104）
   30.1 English-Chinese Translation ……………………………（104）
   30.2 Chinese-English Translation ……………………………（113）

31 2019 年 6 月二级笔译实务真题 ………………………………（117）
   31.1 English-Chinese Translation ……………………………（117）
   31.2 Chinese-English Translation ……………………………（128）

32 2021 年 11 月二级笔译真题 ……（134）
   32.1 English-Chinese Translation ……………………………（134）
   32.2 Chinese-English Translation ……………………………（141）

主要参考文献 ……………………（147）

0 导 论

二级笔译考试中常出现较为复杂的句型结构,如何应对这些结构成了考生心中的难题。市面上现有的解析大多缺乏一个有据可循且可以直接套用的模式。因此,我们以中英文句间逻辑为基础,提出了如下体系:将中英文句子均拆解为主干和定状结构,并根据中英语言差异进行转译处理。

0.1 主 干

英文是形合的语言,再复杂的英文句子都是通过语法手段和逻辑手段连接起来的。因此,理解和翻译英文长难句的关键在于理清句子层次。理清句子层次的第一步是找到句子的主干。

英文句子的主干形式有七种:主语+谓语动词(SV)、主语+谓语动词+补语(SVC)、主语+谓语动词+宾语(SVO)、主语+谓语动词+宾语+补语(SVOC)、主语+谓语动词+间接宾语+直接宾语(SVoO)、主语+谓语动词+状语(SVA)、主语+谓语动词+宾语+状语(SVOA)。

[例·真题] While the battle ended two centuries ago, however, hard feelings have endured.

分析 这句话的主语是 hard feelings,谓语动词是 have endured,为典型的 SV 结构。while 引导让步状语从句。这个让步状语从句的主语是 the battle,谓语动词是 ended,时间状语是 two centuries ago,为 SVA 结构。

中文是意合的语言,确定中文句子的主干至关重要。中文多是流水小句,结构呈竹节式,句子内部以及句子与句子间的逻辑关系通常不明显。因此,中译英的难点在于句子各成分的拆分和排列,可以把所有的中文转变为中文的英文句式,归入上述七种英文句子主干形式。如:

[例·真题] 纵观世界文明史,人类先后经历了农业革命、工业革命、信息革命。

译文 Throughout the history of human civilization, humanity has gone through the Agricultural Revolution, Industrial Revolution and Information Revolution.

分析 这句话的主干转变为中文的英文句式:人类经历了农业革命、工业革命、信息革命。这是典型的 SVO 结构。其中"纵观世界文明史"是时间状语。

0.2 定语与状语

为满足表达的需要,英文句子在主干的基础上往往还有其他成分,即定语、状语、同位语和插入语。这些成分本质上都是修饰语。定语修饰名词和代词。状语修饰形容词、副词、谓语动词和整个句子。同位语对名词和代词进行解释和补充说明。插入语位于一句话中间,借助标点符号与主句分隔开来,既可以作定语也可以作状语。在实际操作中,同位语和插入语可以当作定语或状语进行处理。

(1)英译中的关键在于处理好定语与状语。

定语的处理方式主要有五种:前置、后置、置于句首、合并和转译。一般来讲,如果定语是单词或内部没有过多修饰成分的定语从句,翻译时可将定语放在被修饰成分之前,前置处理;如果定语是修饰成分过多、非常复杂的定语从句,则将定语放在最后单独成句,后置处理;如果定语从句与主句之间存在因果逻辑关系,则将定语从句放在句首,单独成句;如果"there be"句型中包含定语从句,则将定语从句与主语合并,处理成主谓结构,在翻译时省略"there be";如果定语部分不好处理,可采取转译的方法,通常是将它转译为状语(详见本书第5章)。

状语的处理方式也有四种:顺译、倒译、转译和省译。如果按照原文语序进行翻译毫无违和感,则采取顺译的方式处理状语。考虑到中文常按照时序、因果和条件的逻辑展开,而英文的状语位置相对灵活,可将英文中后置的状语部分先翻译,然后再翻译主句,即倒译。如果状语部分不好处理,则可采取转译的方法,通常是将它转译为定语。对于没必要翻译出来的逻辑连词,例如when,可采取省译的方法,只翻译状语从句的内容而不翻译逻辑连词(详见本书第6章)。

(2)中译英的关键在于处理好定语或状语。确定中文主干后可根据逻辑关系将剩余的成分处理成英文中的定语或状语。此外,应根据中英文中定语和状语的位置差异作出适当调整,将较长的定语后置,将状语放在主句后。

0.3 转 译

转译在本质上是一个润色的过程。英文和中文在表述上并不是一一对应的,有时直接按照原文结构翻译会导致行文不通顺、不流畅。在这种情况下,可采取转译的方法使译文符合目的语读者的阅读习惯。

在单词层面上,转译一般发生在名词、动词、形容词和副词之间;而在句子层面上,句子间的各成分之间可以相互转换。如:

[例·真题] Art museums have watched this development nervously, fearing damage to their collections or to visitors, as users swing their sticks with abandon.

译文 在(自拍杆)使用者肆意挥舞自拍杆时,艺术博物馆的人担忧地看着这一情形,生怕伤害到藏品或游客。

分析 art museums have watched this development 是句子的主干,fearing damage to their collections or to visitors,as users swing their sticks with abandon 是原因状语。这个原因状语中还包含有一个时间状语 as users swing their sticks with abandon。其中 damage 可转译为同根动词 damage。

0.4 逻 辑

逻辑包含并列关系和各种从属关系,在翻译时需体现出来。

英文句子的逻辑关系常通过逻辑关系词展现,呈显性的逻辑,且一个完整的句子主干只有确定的一个。如:

[例·真题] A metal fence surrounds the grounds of the archives, and a security guard stands watching at the gate, so there is little risk that local predators—large, unleashed dogs, for instance—will be able to reach the ewes.

译文 金属护栏包围在档案馆四周,还有一名安保人员在门口站岗,因此,不拴绳的大狗等当地大型掠食者很难接近到母羊。

分析 这句话是由两个逻辑连词连接的三个小句组成的,and 表示并列关系,so 表示因果关系。

有时,英文中的并列句也能体现除并列之外的逻辑关系。

[例] It seems that these two branches of science are mutually dependent, and that so-called division between the pure scientist and the applied scientist is more apparent than real.

译文 似乎这两个科学分支互相依存,因为纯粹科学家和应用科学家之间所谓的分界线与其说是真实存在的,不如说是表面上的。

分析 it seems that ...是句子的主干,and 连接的是两个宾语从句。虽然从形式上看这两个宾语从句是并列关系,但是从逻辑关系上看,后一个宾语从句是前一个宾语从句的原因,呈因果逻辑关系。

中文句子通常没有明显的逻辑关系词,呈隐性的连贯。因此,需要依靠原文意思将它转变为中文的英文句式,再根据各小句的逻辑关系确定定语和状语。一个较长且逻辑复杂的中文句子有时可依据逻辑关系拆分出两个或两个以上的句子。

[例·真题] 北京将把全面治理行人及非机动车交通违法行为作为交通秩序整治的重点,通过纠正、教育、批评和处罚等措施治理"中国式过马路"现象。

译文 Beijing will overhaul "Chinese style road crossing" through measures such as correction, education, criticism and fines, with paramount importance attached to rectifying the traffic law violation behaviors of pedestrians and non-motor vehicles.

分析 这句话的主语是"北京",谓语动词是"治理",宾语是"'中国式过马路'现象","把全面治理行人及非机动车交通违法行为作为交通秩序整治的重点"是伴随状语,方式状语是"通过纠正、教育、批评和处罚等措施"。

基础知识篇

1 中英文的差异

中文和英文并不是一一对应的,二者分属两个不同的语系。为提高译文的可读性,译者需考虑到中英文的差异,并以此为依据作出适当调整,使译文符合目的语读者的习惯。中英文的差异主要体现在形式上和表述上。

1.1 形式差异

中英文的形式差异主要体现在句子形态、用词及逻辑关系等方面。从句子形态方面看,中文句子呈竹节状,英文句子呈树状;从用词方面看,中文多用动态词语,英文多用静态词语及结构;从逻辑关系的表现方面看,中文是意合的语言,而英文是形合的语言。

1.1.1 中文竹节,英文树状

汉语的一句话通常由多个小句组成,小句间常常以标点符号连接,且没有逻辑连词,各小句之间的逻辑关系是隐性的。因此,中文的句子形态是竹节状的。

[例·真题]互联网让世界变成了"鸡犬之声相闻"的地球村,相隔万里的人们不再"老死不相往来"。

译文 The Internet has turned the world into a global village so that distance no longer prevents people from interacting with each other.

分析 这句话由两个呈因果逻辑关系的小句组成,其间没有逻辑连词,在翻译时需把隐含在句间的逻辑关系通过 so that 体现出来。

英文句子中的各成分都是通过语法手段和逻辑手段连接起来的,各成分之间的逻辑关系明显,呈树状形态。

[例·真题] A rambling though dilapidated farmstead called Hougoumont, which was crucial to the battle's outcome, is being painstakingly restored as an education center.

译文 霍高蒙特(Hougoumont)是此次战役成败的关键,如今,人们正煞费苦心地将这座广袤却破败的农庄修复成一个教育中心。

分析 a farmstead is being painstakingly restored 是句子的主干;rambling though dilapidated 是定语,被用来修饰主语;called Hougoumont 是后置定语,被用来修饰主语;which 引导非限定定语从句,被用来修饰 Hougoumont;as an education center 是主语补语。

以主干为基础,分词、定语从句、补语等结构使句意更加完整。定语从句与主句呈因果逻辑关系,在翻译时置于句首处理。

1.1.2　中文动态,英文静态

中英文的另一大差异体现在动静上。中文是动态的语言,善用动词;英文是静态的语言,善用名词和介词短语。

在中译英时,可采用"谓语动词的过渡"这一方式,将动词转译为名词,并补充弱动词作谓语动词。在处理"副词+谓语动词"结构时,也可以将副词转译为动词,将谓语动词转译为名词,从而实现谓语动词的过渡。

在英译中时,可将有动词词根的抽象名词转译为同根动词,并将介词短语等静态成分处理成动词词组,也可以直接省译弱动词,即谓语动词的过渡词,只翻译实义动词。

[例·真题] 目前,西藏已经深深融入全国统一的市场体系,来自全国和世界各地的商品源源不断地进入西藏,丰富着城乡市场和百姓生活。

译文 Tibet has now become a deeply integrated part of the national market system, commodities from around the country and the world flowing into the province, thus enriching the urban and rural markets as well as people's lives.

分析 句中的"融入""来自""进入""丰富"均是动词,充分体现了中文是动态语言的特征。在翻译时,可将①"融入"转译为名词(an integrated part),并补充弱动词 has become 作为谓语动词,②"来自"处理成介词短语,③"进入"和"丰富"处理成非谓语结构,从而更加符合英文静态语言的表述习惯。

[例·真题] Until the Belitung find, historians had thought that Tang China traded primarily through the land routes of Central Asia, mainly on the Silk Road.

译文 在发现勿里洞沉船之前,历史学家认为唐朝时期中国主要通过丝绸之路上的中亚陆路通道开展对外贸易。

分析 find、through the land routes 和 on the Silk Road 是静态的名词和介词短语,充分体现了英文是静态语言的特征。在翻译时,可将 find 处理成同根动词,可将介词短语处理成动词短语。

1.1.3　中文意合,英文形合

因为中文句子多流水小句,小句间的逻辑关系并没有通过逻辑连词标明,而是通过语意内部的逻辑衔接起来的,所以中文是意合的语言。与中文不同,英文的逻辑关系是显性的,句子与句子之间及句子内部的逻辑关系通过逻辑连词和语法手段清晰地呈现出来,所以英文是形合的语言。在中译英时,要挖掘并体现出逻辑;在英译中时,则要根据原文的逻辑关系断句,并隐去没有必要翻译的逻辑连词。

[例·真题] 中国是世界上最大的发展中国家,人口多,底子薄,经济发展不平衡。

译文 China is the largest developing country in the world, with a large population, a weak foundation and uneven economic development.

分析 句子的主干:中国是世界上最大的发展中国家。"人口多,底子薄,经济发展不平衡"在形态上与主句并列,但实则是对主句的解释说明,所以处理为原因状语。

[例·真题] Steve Jobs established Apple University as a way to inculcate employees into Apple's business culture and educate them about its history, particularly as the company grew and the tech business changed.

译文 特别是随着苹果公司的发展壮大以及科技行业的变化,史蒂夫·乔布斯创立了"苹果大学"来让员工学习苹果的企业文化和发展历史。

分析 Steve Jobs established Apple University 是句子的主干;as a way 是宾语补语;to inculcate employees into Apple's business culture and educate them about its history 是后置定语,被用来修饰宾语补语;particularly as the company grew and the tech business changed 是 as 引导的时间状语从句。在翻译时,需通过"随着"体现句子内部的逻辑关系。

1.2 表述差异

除了形态差异,中英文之间还存在表述差异。这些表述差异体现在主要内容在句中的位置、信息的排列方式以及人称和物称的使用之上。一般来讲,中文前轻后重,英文前重后轻;中文先分后总,英文先总后分;中文善用人称,英文善用物称。

1.2.1 中文前轻后重,英文前重后轻

所谓句子重心就是用于传达句子主要信息(如主谓核心信息)的语言成分。一般来讲,中英文句子的语义重心落在结论、结果、观点、态度或事实等上。然而,中英文句子重心的位置却不同。英文常将句子重心放在句首,开门见山;而中文则将句子重心放在句尾。

[例·真题] 北京交管部门对态度蛮横、拒不服从纠正、有妨碍民警执行公务甚至是袭警行为的违法人员,将坚决依法严格进行处理。

译文 In accordance with law, the Beijing Traffic Administration Bureau will strictly deal with those who act in an unruly manner, refuse to accept correction, obstruct the police's performance of duty and even physically attack the police.

分析 本句话的重心是"将坚决依法严格进行处理"。"对态度蛮横、拒不服从纠正、有妨碍民警执行公务甚至是袭警行为的违法人员"是"处理"的对象,属于次要信息。因为中文的主要信息常放句尾,而英文的主要信息常放句首,所以在中译英时应先翻译句子重心,把次要

成分处理成被定语从句修饰的宾语。

[例·真题] The slopes, first reported in 2011, appear during the warm summer months on Mars, then vanish when the temperatures drop.

译文 2011年,这些斜坡首次出现在报道中,它们于温暖的夏季出现在火星上,然后在温度骤降的时候从火星上消失。

分析 句子的主干:the slopes appear, then vanish。first reported in 2011 是插入语,被用来修饰主语,in 2011、during the warm summer months 和 when the temperatures drop 是时间状语;on Mars 是地点状语。插入语可译为主谓结构。该句重点在于谓语动词 appear 和 vanish。appear 后面接时间状语和地点状语,在翻译时,应遵循中文表达习惯,先译时间状语,再译地点状语,最后译重心部分。vanish 后面接的是时间状语,在翻译时应该先译时间状语,再译重心部分。

1.2.2 中文先分后总,英文先总后分

中英文的信息排列方式存在差异。一般来讲,中文先分说后总结。中文往往遵照逻辑推理的过程,先因后果,先叙事后表态,先条件后结果。在列举时,中文常常先说例子,再陈述例子所属范围。英文则不同。英文习惯于将句子重点前置,所以往往先总结后分说,先表态后叙事,先果后因。在列举时,英文常常先说例子所属的大类再列举。因此,翻译时要作出适当调整,以符合目的语读者的习惯。

[例·真题] 人口的急剧增长,社会经济的迅速发展,给资源和环境带来了空前压力。

译文 The sharp increase of population and the rapid development of society and economy exerted huge pressure on resources and the environment.

分析 句子的主干:增长和发展给资源和环境带来了压力。"人口的""急剧""社会经济的""迅速"和"空前"都是定语。本句话由三个流水小句组成,前两小句与后一小句呈因果逻辑关系,符合中文先分后总的行文习惯。

[例·真题] Each semester I hope, and fear, that I will have nothing to teach my students because they already know how to write.

译文 每个学期,我既满怀希望,又时常担忧,因为学生已经知道如何写作,所以我担心会没什么可教的。

分析 句子的主干是 I hope, and fear that...。each semester 是时间状语。that 引导宾语从句。在这个宾语从句中,I will have nothing 是主干;to teach my students 是后置定语,被用来修饰 nothing;because 引导原因状语从句。这句话先表态,并且先说结果后说原因,符合英文先总后分的行文习惯。

1.2.3　中文善用人称，英文善用物称

中英两种语言的另一差异便是人称与物称的使用。人称（personal subject），即有灵主语，是指有生命的人或动物作其逻辑动词的主语；而物称（impersonal subject），亦无灵主语，是指用无生命的、抽象的事物或概念作部分动词的主语。中文多使用人称，表明人及其行为或状态；而英文多使用物称，在书面语中更为客观。

英中互译时，可将人称与物称灵活转换。中文的无主语句式也可以将物称作主语处理成被动结构，而英文中的非人称代词 it 和"there be"结构也可以转换成汉语的无主语句式。

[例·真题] 在贺兰山腹地，共发现 20 余处遗存岩画。

译文　A total of over 20 relics sites of preserved rock paintings were discovered in the central Helan Mountains.

分析　这句话的主干：发现遗存岩画。"在贺兰山腹地"是地点状语。这是一个隐称无主句，可将原本的宾语"遗存岩画"这一物称作主语，并采用被动结构进行处理。

[例·真题] It's one thing to take a picture at arm's length, but when it is three times arm's length, you are invading someone else's personal space.

译文　伸出胳膊自拍是一回事，但如果是使用三倍于臂长的设备拍照，你就侵犯了他人的私人空间。

分析　句子的主干：to take a picture at arm's length is one thing, but you are invading someone else's personal space. 第一个 it 是形式主语，真正的主语是后面的不定式结构。when 引导条件状语从句，其中的 it 也是一个非人称代词。可将这句话处理为中文的隐称无主句。

2　中英文句子的主干及修饰

在中英文中,所有的句子都可以拆分为主干和修饰两个部分。英文存在七种主干形式,也可以把所有的中文转变为中文的英文句式,归入这七种主干形式。

2.1　主　干

句子的主干由主语(subject)、谓语动词(verb)、宾语(object)、补语(complement)和状语(adverbial)构成。

1. 主语+谓语动词(SV)

英文的 SV 结构:Danny disappears。

同理,中文也同样可以提取出 SV 结构。

[例·真题] 1882 年中国第一盏电灯在上海点亮。

译文 In 1882, China's first electric lamp was turned on.(注:二级笔译的真题中很少有纯粹的 SV 结构,为了方便阐述,这里省略了状语。)

分析 句子的主干转变为中文的英文句式:电灯点亮在上海。忽略状语"在上海",主干可浓缩为:电灯点亮。这是典型的 SV 结构。

2. 主语+谓语动词+补语(SVC)

从严格意义来讲,主语补语是用于补充说明主语的结果、程度、状态、数量、目的等的成分,因此,"主语+系动词+表语"这种结构应为 SVC 结构。

英文的 SVC 结构:This problem is difficult to solve。

同理,中文也同样可以提取出 SVC 结构。

[例·真题] 中国也成为白炽灯的生产和消费大国。

译文 China has become a major producer and consumer of incandescent lamps.

分析 句子的主干:中国成为生产和消费大国。这是典型的 SVC 结构。

3. 主语+谓语动词+宾语(SVO)

英文的 SVO 结构:No one drives the car。

同理,中文也同样可以提取出 SVO 结构。

[例·真题] 它不仅传承着源远流长的古代文明。

译文 It not only carries the long-standing ancient civilization.

分析 这句话节选自段落中的一个分句,这句话的主干转变为中文的英文句式:它传承着文明。这是典型的SVO结构。

4. 主语＋谓语动词＋宾语＋补语(SVOC)

在SVOC结构中,宾语补足语的中心词是宾语,对宾语的结果、程度、状态、数量、目的等进行补充说明。宾语补语与宾语之间的关系较为紧密,去掉补语可能会导致句意的缺失。

英文的SVOC结构:We all want you happy。

同理,中文也同样可以提取出SVOC结构。

[例] 我们发现相对论很难解释。

译文 We find that the theory of relativity difficult to explain.

分析 这句话的主干部分就是很典型的SVOC结构,"我们"为主语,"发现"为谓语动词,"相对论"为宾语,"很难解释"为宾补(对宾语进行补充说明)。

5. 主语＋谓语动词＋间接宾语＋直接宾语(SVoO)

在双宾语结构中,能充当间接宾语或是直接宾语的一般是名词或代词。与宾补相比,其成分选择较为单一。两个宾语之间的关系有时较为松散,去掉其中一个宾语,有的句子依然可以成立。

英文的SVoO结构:Tom gave his mother a big hug。

同理,中文也同样可以提取出SVoO结构。

[例] 老人正在给孩子们讲长征时候的故事。

译文 The old man is telling the children stories in the Long March.

分析 这句话中的主干部分就是典型的SVoO结构,"孩子们"是间接宾语,"故事"是直接宾语。

6. 主语＋谓语动词＋状语(SVA)

这种结构有时候由于谓语动词的特殊性,后面必须加状语成分,否则句子结构不完整,导致句意缺失。

英文的SVA结构:Jenny will travel on Monday(on Monday为时间状语,可省略,不影响句意),We live in China(in China为地点状语,不能省略,否则句意缺失)。

同理,中文也同样可以提取出SVA结构。

[例] 他的父母在这家公司工作十年了。

译文 His parents have worked in the company for ten years.

分析 这句话中的主干部分是"他的父母工作","在这家公司"作地点状语,"十年"为时间状语,整体来看就是典型的SVA结构。

7. 主语＋谓语动词＋宾语＋状语(SVOA)

在 SVOA 句式中,有时候需要通过添加状语的方式来表达时间、地点或目的等,否则会导致句意的不完整。

英文的 SVOA 结构:I will make her a cake tomorrow(tomorrow 为时间状语,可省略,不影响句意),I put the book on the desk(on the desk 为地点状语,不可省略,否则影响句意)。

同理,中文也同样可以提取出 SVA 结构。

[例·真题] 通过对话和协商,以和平方式解决国际争端。

译文 We should settle international disputes in peace through dialogue and consultation.

分析 把这句话的主干转变为中文的英文句式:我们解决国际争端,以和平的方式,通过对话和协商。这句话的转换关键是补充主语"我们"。"以和平的方式"和"通过对话和协商"均可处理成方式状语。这是典型的 SVOA 结构。

2.2 修饰语

为了将一件事描述得更为具体、详尽,在主干的基础上,可以添加一些修饰语,如定语、状语、同位语和插入语。

2.2.1 定语

定语是用来修饰、限定、说明名词或代词的相关品质与特征的成分,可以是形容词、数量词、名词、代词或从句等。根据在句中位置的不同,它可分为前置定语和后置定语。在翻译过程中,它通常有三种处理方式,即前置译法、后置译法和句首译法。

[例] Both picnics and barbeques are friendly, informal social events that offer an opportunity to enjoy a meal outside in pleasant surroundings.

译文 野餐和烧烤都是友情洋溢、不拘礼节的社交活动,可以让大家在户外怡情的环境里高高兴兴地美餐一顿。(定语从句的后置处理)

2.2.2 状语

状语也是一种修饰语,修饰的是动词、形容词和整个句子。在形态上,状语可以是单词、介词短语、非谓语、独立主格或从句。状语可分为修饰性状语、连接性状语、评注性状语三大类。其中修饰性状语又可以分为时间状语、地点状语、方式状语、原因状语、目的状语、条件状语、结果状语、让步状语、比较状语、伴随状语和解释状语,共十一种。

[例] By extending their abilities through cooperation in pursuit of common goals, individuals secure for themselves and each other a basic or minimum state of well-being.

译文 在追求共同目标的过程中,个体通过合作延展能力,从而为自己和彼此获得了一种基本的或最低程度的幸福状态。(翻译时体现出了方式状语。)

2.2.3 同位语

同位语用于对另一个名词或代词进行解释或补充说明。在翻译过程中,它通常可以被处理成定语和状语的形式,也可以译为主谓句。

[例] Coincident with concerns about the accelerating loss of species and habitats has been a growing appreciation of the importance of biological diversity, the number of species in a particular ecosystem, to the health of the earth and human well-being.

译文1 人们越来越担忧物种及其栖息地的加速流失问题,与此同时,人们越来越认识到生物多样性——一个特定生态系统中的物种数量——对于地球健康和人类福祉的重要性。

译文2 生物多样性是在一个特定生态系统中的物种数量,人们越来越意识到其对地球健康和人类福祉的重要性,与此同时,人们越来越担忧物种及其栖息地的加速流失问题。

分析 观察译文,同位语的形式除了添加破折号这种基本的形式来体现,还可以译为主谓结构。

2.2.4 插入语

插入语可以用于补充句意,从而使句子更加完整。它始终位于句子中间,用逗号或破折号隔开。在翻译时,它一般被处理成定语或状语形式。

[例] This matter, frankly speaking, has nothing to do with me.

译文 坦白地讲,这件事和我一点关系都没有。(插入语为评注性状语。)

3 定 语

定语，即名词修饰语，常用于修饰、限定或说明名词、代词等的性质与特征。根据在句中位置的不同，它可以分为前置定语和后置定语。根据其功能的不同，它可以分为限制性定语和非限制性定语。

3.1 定语的类型

定语在中英文中都存在，且类型多样，可以是名词、形容词、分词、短语或句子。其中短语包括介词结构和不定式等。英文中的定语形式变化更为灵活，故本小节的例子均以英文为主。

3.1.1 名词

[例·真题] The dean demurred, but Mr. Silver, a <u>fellow graduate</u> student who overheard their conversation, was intrigued.

3.1.2 形容词

[例·真题] <u>Curious</u> humans, however, are encouraged to visit the sheep.

3.1.3 分词

[例·真题] The sheep, from a rare, diminutive Breton breed <u>called Quessant</u>, stand just about two feet high.

3.1.4 短语

[例·真题] Museums <u>across the United States</u> have been imposing bans on using selfie sticks for photographs inside galleries.

3.1.5 句子

[例·真题] The Metropolitan Museum of Art, <u>which has been studying the matter for some time</u>, has just decided that it will forbid selfie slicks.

3.2 定语的位置

在句子中,定语的位置通常有两种,即在中心词之前或之后。根据在句子中位置的不同,它可以分为前置定语和后置定语。二者有时可以相互转换。前置定语包括所有出现在中心词之前的修饰成分;后置定语则包括所有出现在中心词之后的修饰成分。

[例·真题] The pesticide was banned this year for use on many flowering crops in Europe that attract honey bees.

分析 在名词词组 many flowering crops in Europe that attract honey bees 中,既存在前置定语,又存在后置定语。形容词 many flowering 为前置定语,修饰中心词 crops;介词短语 in Europe 和从句 that attract honey bees 为后置定语,也修饰中心词 crops。

3.3 定语的功能

定语与其中心词整体构成名词词组。从定语与中心词语义关系的角度来讲,定语的功能有限制性和非限制性之分。限制性定语规定名词词组的所指意义,与中心词在语义上有着不可分割的联系;非限制性修饰语只是起到补充说明中心词的作用,其本身并不影响整个名词词组的所指意义。前置定语和后置定语都有限制性和非限制性的功能之分,后置定语的这两种功能更容易区分。

3.3.1 前置定语的限制性与非限制性

一般来讲,凡是带有对比性质的前置定语都是限制性定语。

[例·真题] Apple may well be the only technical company on the planet.

分析 在名词词组 the only technical company on the planet 中,the only 和 technical 均为限制性定语,被用来修饰中心词 company。technical 表示 company 的类别,是技术公司而不是互联网公司;the only 表示 company 的性质是唯一一家,而不是其中一家。

[例·真题] China is a well-known beautiful country.

分析 在名词词组 a well-known beautiful country 中,well-known 如果不是特指与不出名的美丽国家相比,就是非限制性定语,不代表 country 的本质特征,省略后不影响句意,而 beautiful 则是限制性定语,被用来修饰中心词 country。

3.3.2 后置定语的限制性与非限制性

后置定语的不同功能在形式上主要体现在中心词和定语之间是否存在","。若两者之间没有","，则该后置定语为限制性定语；若两者之间以","隔开，则该后置定语为非限制性定语。

[例·真题] The last image is a curvy stick figure that is still unmistakably a bull.

分析 在这句话中，that is still unmistakably a bull 为限制性定语从句，被用来修饰中心词 figure。

[例·真题] The Metropolitan Museum of Art, which has been studying the matter for some time, has just decided that it will forbid selfie slicks.

分析 在这句话中，which has been studying the matter for some time 为非限制性定语从句，被用来修饰中心词 the Metropolitan Museum of Art。

需要注意的是，从严格意义上来讲，定语限制性功能与非限制性功能的界定并不清晰，二者在实际中往往难以区分，尤其是在分隔修饰的情况中。

[例·真题] The teacher borrowed a megaphone from her colleague, which helps the class listen more clearly.

分析 在这句话中，which 引导的定语从句本应紧跟中心词 megaphone 之后，但却被介词短语 from her colleague 分隔开来。这就导致 which 的先行词不够明确，容易被误认为是 her colleague，从而导致歧义。

在某些情况下，分隔修饰的存在是必要的。

[例·真题] Laura Andreessen, a philanthropist and lecturer on philanthropy at Stanford who has been close friends with Ms. Powell Jobs for two decades.

分析 在该分句中，a philanthropist and lecturer 的定语从句 who has been close friends with Ms. Powell Jobs for two decades 被另一个定语 on philanthropy at Stanford 分隔开来。如果将 on philanthropy at Stanford 置于定语从句 who has been close friends with Ms. Powell Jobs for two decades 之后，其修饰意义就会发生变化，从而导致语义歧义。

[例·真题] Her philanthropic work, especially on education causes like College Track, the college preparatory organization she helped found and through which she was Ms. Castro's mentor, has been her priority and focus.

分析 这句话的插入语部分为 especially on education causes like College Track，其中 the college preparatory organization 是 College Track 的同位语。这个同位语又跟了两个并列定语从句 she helped found 和 through which she was Ms. Castro's mentor。

[例] The only choice is to attempt to make as reasonable a story as I can of this novel which I have written for ten months.

分析 在这句话中,中心词 a story 被嵌入一个比较结构 as reasonable... as I can 之中,并成为一个不可分割的整体,故而它的后置定语 of this novel... 只能放在比较结构之后,形成分隔修饰。

在上述三种情况中,分隔修饰便是可取的。反之,如果毫无理由地将定语与其中心词分隔开来,通常会造成病句。

4 状　语

状语(adverbial)也是一种修饰语,常被用来修饰动词、形容词、副词或整个句子。在形态上,状语可以是单词(如 importantly)、介词短语、非谓语结构、独立主格结构,还可以是句子(即状语从句)。状语在中英文中的位置有所不同。在中文中,状语常置于句首或主语之后。在英文中,状语有三种情况:单词,常放在被修饰成分之前;短语(介词短语、非谓语结构、独立主格结构),常放在句首或被修饰成分之后;状语从句,既可以放在主句之前也可以放在主句之后,但考虑到中英文差异,状语从句多出现在主句之后。

4.1 修饰性状语

修饰性状语共有十一种:时间状语、地点状语、方式状语、条件状语、原因状语、结果状语、目的状语、让步状语、比较状语、伴随状语、解释状语。前面九种状语修饰的是谓语动词,与九种状语从句一一对应,这里不作详述。伴随状语和解释状语则比较特殊。一般来讲,伴随状语与主句的谓语动词发生几乎同步,而解释状语则是对主句的谓语动词进行进一步的解释说明。

[例] According to this theory, our early life experiences, with parents responsible for our well-being, are at the root of our attachment to the adults with whom we form close relationships.

分析 according to this theory 是原因状语;with parents responsible for our well-being 是独立主格结构,与 early life experiences 的 are 在时间、意义上一致,为伴随状语。这个独立主格结构的逻辑主语是 parents,与主句主语不同,它修饰的是 are。

[例] We redoubled our efforts, each man working like two.

分析 each man working like two 在形式上是独立主格,对 redoubled 作出解释,为解释状语。

4.2 评注性状语

评注性状语带有作者的主观感情,体现着作者的看法,修饰的是整个句子。

[例] Fortunately, he accomplished the mission on time.

> **分析** fortunately 体现了作者的情感态度,是评注性状语。

此外,评注性状语还可以表示某个领域。

> [例] In the field of biology, he is an expert.

> **分析** in the field of biology 指明了领域,是评注性状语。

4.3　连接性状语

连接性状语起着连接本句话与上一句话的作用,修饰的是整个句子。

> [例·真题] Still, there are some very old farms out there.

> **分析** still 衔接本句话与上句话,表明本句话与上文存在转折关系,是连接性状语。

> [例·真题] In the end, the scientists concluded that 63 percent of saltwater fish stocks had been depleted "below what we think of as a target range," Dr. Worm said.

> **分析** in the end 承接上文,表明本句话是前一句话描述的行为步骤之一,是连接性状语。

英译中的主要技巧有定语的处理、状语的处理、同位语和插入语的处理、转译的处理、逻辑的处理、长句的处理，其他技巧有词和表达的选择、被动语态的处理、增减的处理、数词的处理、专有名词的处理。

5 定 语

在英文中,定语的形式多样,并且经常会出现词句并列或套用的情况,导致修饰成分十分复杂;而在中文中,除了某种特殊的修辞需要外,定语总是位于所修饰的词语前,这也就表明汉语中的前置定语不会太长。因此,在英译中的过程中,英文定语成分的处理需要采取灵活的翻译方法,如前置处理、后置处理、句首处理、合并处理、转译处理、语序调整处理。

5.1 前 置

一般来说,如果英文定语成分是较短的短语和从句等,可以采用前置译法,将定语部分放置在其中心词前面进行翻译。

[例·真题] It shows us that the world in the ninth century was not as fragmented as we assumed.

译文 它告诉我们 9 世纪时的世界并没有我们想得那么封闭隔绝。

分析 在这句话中,in the ninth century 为定语,修饰中心词 the world,因词数较短,因此在翻译过程中可以采取前置的处理方法,不会影响整体句意。

[例·真题] Manuel Tritschler, 28, a third-generation beekeeper who works for Bayer.

译文 28 岁的曼纽尔·崔施乐是在拜耳工作的第三代养蜂人。

分析 在这句话中,who 引导限制性定语从句,被用来修饰中心词 Manuel Tritschler。因句式较短,定语从句可翻译成"在拜耳工作的",置于中心词前,使汉语句子变成表意清晰的简单句。

5.2 后 置

当英语句子里的定语成分较长时,如定语从句,一般可以采取后置译法,将它拆分为整句中的并列小句,置于其原有修饰词之后,单独翻译出来。需要注意的是,在此类情况中,有时可能会根据句子的意思,在该后置小句中重复一下其原有先行词,使用人称代词或者指示代词等来衔接前后句的逻辑关系。

[例·真题] The sea-cucumber divers who found the wreck had no idea it eventually would be considered one of the most important maritime discoveries of the late 20th century.

译文 这艘沉船的残骸是捕捞海参的潜水员发现的,但他们怎么也不会想到,这一发现竟会被视为 20 世纪晚期最重要的海上发现之一。

分析 这句话中存在多处定语成分。翻译时主要看后半部分的定语从句 it eventually would be considered… 如何处理。该定语从句省略引导词 that,修饰中心词 idea。由于定语词数过多,前置翻译会使中文句子结构过于冗长,故可以采用后置的翻译方法,让句子结构更为清晰。

5.3 句 首

句首译法就是将定语从句完全置于整个句子的前面,使之单独成句,从而起到调整句子语序的效果。在应用时,主语和定语从句之间往往存在较为明显的逻辑关系,其中以因果关系较为常见。

[例·真题] The oil industry that at one stage sparked talk of Scotland as "the Kuwait of the West" has already outlived most predictions.

译文 阿伯丁的石油产业曾一度激发了苏格兰是"西方苏威特"的讨论。这种繁华已经超出了大部分人的预期。

分析 在这句话中,that 引导的限制性定语从句修饰中心词 oil industry,且和主句存在一定的因果关系。由于主语过长,为使句意更加流畅,可以采取句首译法,将名词性短语译为一个完整的句子,即"阿伯丁的石油产业曾一度激发了苏格兰是'西方苏威特'的讨论",并置于句首。

5.4 合 并

合并译法是指在符合前后句语义表达的基础上,将主句和定语从句的主干信息合并到一起,使译文简洁易懂。在通常情况下,合并译法可以应用于两种情况:一种是 there be 句型中的宾语和修饰它的限制性定语从句的相应成分融合在一起;另一种则是由于原句中修饰性成分过长,在翻译时合并处理为主谓结构。

[例·真题] There are very few diseases that people get from worms.

译文 很少有疾病是从蠕虫那里感染的。

分析 这句话是 there be 结构引出的句子。在这种句型当中,可以将句子中的宾语 very few diseases 和修饰它的定语从句 that people get from worms 进行合并处理。

[例·真题] Randy Nelson, who came from the animation studio Pixar, co-founded by Mr. Jobs, is one of the teachers of "Communicating at Apple".

译文 兰迪·纳尔逊（Randy Nelson）曾就职于乔布斯与他人合作创立的皮克斯动画工作室，现在是"在苹果学沟通"这门课程的讲师之一。

分析 在这句话中，who 引导非限制性定语从句，修饰中心词 Randy Nelson。作为主语的名词性短语过长，可以将英语原句的主句和定语从句融合成一个简单句，即"兰迪·纳尔逊曾就职于乔布斯与他人合作创立的皮克斯动画工作室"，打乱原有结构和语序，从而凸显句子的主要信息。

5.5 转 译

在定语从句的翻译中，转译处理主要是指定语、状语之间的转换，但其实这种转译还是具有任意性的，需要根据具体的句意进行判断，看是否需要转译成其他成分，如动词或名词等。

[例] By extending their abilities through cooperation in pursuit of common goals, individuals secure for themselves and each other a basic or minimum state of well-being.

译文 在追求共同目标的过程中，个体通过合作延伸能力，从而为自己和彼此获得了一种基本的或最低程度的幸福状态。

分析 在这句话中，in pursuit of common goals 为定语，修饰中心词 cooperation。为保证句意的流畅，在翻译时可转译为时间状语，即"在追求共同目标的过程中"。

[例·真题] Dating from 1534, the inn, now called Shakespeare House, is thought to have been built as a Tudor hunting lodge.

译文 这座旅馆现在被称为"莎士比亚之屋"，始建于1534年，被认为曾是都铎王朝时期的狩猎小屋。

分析 在这句话中，分词短语 now called Shakespeare House 为定语，修饰中心词 inn。由于分词存在动词词根，为保证句意的流畅，在翻译时可转译为动词，即"称作"。

5.6 语序调整

语序指句子单词或成分的先后排列顺序，包括词序和句序。在定语的翻译过程中，经常会涉及到词序的变化，如多个形容词的排序、of 结构等。以下将主要介绍定语处理过程中的词序调整处理。

5.6.1 形容词修饰语的排序

在英文句子中，中心词前可能有多个形容词修饰语。英文修饰语一般遵循以下从前到后的排序：限定词、描述性词、大小、形状、条件、新旧、颜色、来源、材料。在英译汉时，需要根据语义对多个形容词修饰语的排序进行灵活调整。

[例·真题] All because a bright young man, his mind ablaze with dots and dashes, one day raked his fingers through the sand.

译文 这一切都是因为一个聪明的年轻人脑中充满了点与线的思考，某天他用手指划过了沙子。

[例] It offers a lot of market opportunities for manufactures all over the world and is still constantly looking for new, effective and economical products and services worldwide.

译文 它为世界各地的制造商提供了很多市场机会，并依然坚持不懈地在全球范围内寻找有效而经济的新产品和新服务。

5.6.2 of 结构

英文句子中经常会使用 of 结构对中心词进行限定，当句子中出现形容词＋中心名词＋of＋名词的结构时，需要根据语义对形容词修饰语和 of 后修饰语进行排序。翻译成中文时的顺序通常为形容词＋名词＋中心名词。

[例·真题] Outside the cozy two-story building that houses the center is a whimsical yellow sculpture of a bee.

译文 在这座舒适的两层小楼外面，有一个造型奇特的黄色蜜蜂雕塑。

分析 在这句话中，中心词为 sculpture，中心词前的定语为 whimsical 和 yellow，根据形容词排序，应先说描述性词，再说颜色词，即"造型奇特的黄色"。of 后的名词与中心词的关系最为密切，在译文中位置也应最紧密，根据语序顺序，可将整个名词词组译为"造型奇特的黄色蜜蜂雕塑"。

6 状　语

状语是句子的一个重要修饰成分,可修饰动词、形容词和整个句子,从时间、方式、条件、范围和程度等方面对中心词进行修饰、限制。状语可分为修饰性状语、连接性状语、评注性状语三大类,在句中的位置比较灵活,常见于句首或者句尾,还可置于句中作为插入成分或是补充说明成分。由于状语的形式多样,所以在翻译时可根据上下文以及汉语表达的需要灵活选用不同的方法,如顺译法、倒译法、转译法、省译法等。

6.1 顺　译

顺译法是指在英译中时,不用对状语的位置进行大的变动,译成中文后,其本身的位置对应到汉语中正好符合中文的表达规范,以便译文读起来流畅、地道。

[例·真题] For nations in Europe, be they small or large, literature will always be one of the keys of their cultural existence, and we recognize that this is the only way we are going to be able to make that literature present in the United States.

译文 对欧洲各国而言,无论国家大小,文学将一直是各国文化的核心要素,我们也认识到,上述举措是让欧洲文学立足美国的唯一必由之路。

分析 在这句话中,让步状语 be they small or large 的位置不用进行调整,翻译成中文后按照原来的位置放在句中读起来也十分自然流畅,可直接采用顺译法。

6.2 倒　译

为满足汉语表达习惯,有时要对状语的位置进行灵活调整,可置于句首或句尾。

[例·真题] Despite that far-flung status, Madeira catapulted into the center of the Union's agricultural and environmental affairs last year when Portugal asked the European Commission for permission to impose an unprecedented ban on growing biotech crops there.

译文 去年葡萄牙向欧盟委员会提出申请,要在马德拉群岛实施一项前所未有的禁令,即禁止当地种植转基因作物。这让原本远离欧洲大陆的马德拉群岛迅速成为了欧盟农业和环境问题的焦点。

分析 在这句话中,时间状语从句 when Portugal asked the European Commission for permission to impose an unprecedented ban on growing biotech crops there 表明事件背景，为符合汉语表达习惯，通常被置于句首，故翻译时采用倒译法。

6.3 转　译

考虑到汉语表述和逻辑的要求，有些状语需要转译。在通常情况下，可将状语转译为定语。

[例·真题] In "What Makes Apple, Apple", another course that Mr. Nelson occasionally teaches, he showed a slide of the remote control for the Google TV.

译文　尼尔森偶尔也会讲授另一门课程"是什么造就了苹果"，并在课上展示了一张谷歌电视遥控器的幻灯片。

分析　这句话中出现了多处转译。地点状语 in "What Makes Apple, Apple"转译为定语，修饰中心名词 another course，使译文表达更加符合中文逻辑。

6.4 省　译

省译法指的是在翻译状语成分时省略关联词，从而使汉语译文的表达更为简洁紧凑。

[例·真题] The runaway success of Stieg Larsson's *Millennium* trilogy suggests that when it comes to contemporary literature in translation, Americans are at least willing to read Scandinavian detective fiction.

译文　斯蒂格·拉森(Stieg Larsson)的《千禧年》三部曲大获成功，表明在现代文学翻译作品中，美国读者至少还愿意阅读来自斯堪的纳维亚的侦探小说。

分析　这句话在翻译时省略了时间状语从句引导词 when 的翻译，直接交代了从句的核心句意，即"在现代文学翻译作品当中"，使译文更加紧凑。

7 同位语和插入语

除了定语和状语外,英文中还有两种修饰语,即同位语和插入语。

7.1 同位语

同位语是对中心词作解释说明和补充的修饰成分。同位语在句中的位置相对灵活:它既可以紧跟在被修饰成分之后,也可以通过标点符号与主句隔开,即作插入语,还可以通过其他成分与被修饰成分分隔开来,呈分割结构。在形态上,同位语可以是名词词组,也可以是同位语从句。同位语从句的引导词有三类:连词 that、whether,连接代词 what、who,连接副词 why、when、where。

[例·真题] All this despite the fact that weddings (and marriages in general, honestly) can be a fairly impractical thing to invest in.

分析 that 引导同位语从句,解释说明 fact,紧跟在 fact 之后。

[例·真题] Every year, in districts of Wallonia, the French-speaking part of Belgium, there are fetes to honor Napoleon, according to Count Georges Jacobs de Hagen, a prominent Belgian industrialist and chairman of a committee responsible for restoring Hougoumont.

分析 the French-speaking part of Belgium 在形态上是插入语,实则是同位语,解释说明了 Wallonia。此外,a prominent Belgian industrialist and chairman of a committee responsible for restoring Hougoumont 也是一个同位语,解释说明了 Count Georges Jacobs de Hagen。

[例·真题] Her finding, published in *Nature* in 1964, that chimpanzees use tools extracting insects from a termite mound with leaves of grass—drastically and forever altered humanity's understanding of itself.

分析 that 引导的同位语从句解释说明 finding,为避免头重脚轻放在句尾,由作后置定语的插入语与被修饰成分分隔开来。

因为同位语与定语都是名词和代词的修饰成分,所以,同位语的处理方法可参照本书第 5 章。此外,同位语还可以转换为主谓结构,或作顶针处理。顶针译法本质上是重译法,即重复中心词,目的是让译文更顺畅。

[例·真题] The sea-cucumber divers who found the wreck had no idea it eventually would be considered one of the most important maritime discoveries of the late 20th century.

[译文] 发现沉船的捞参渔民并不知道,勿里洞沉船最终会被人们视作20世纪晚期最重要的海洋考古发现之一。

[分析] 句子的主干为 the sea-cucumber divers had no idea。who found the wreck 是定语从句,修饰主语。it eventually would be considered one of the most important maritime discoveries of the late 20th century 是 idea 的同位语从句。英译中时可将这个较长的同位语从句处理为主谓结构,并将 idea 转译为动词"知道",与主谓结构相配合。

[例·真题] **He believed in a hypothesis first put forth by Charles Darwin that humans and chimpanzees share an evolutionary ancestor.**

[译文] 他相信一个首先由查尔斯·达尔文提出的假说,这个假说认为人类和大猩猩有相同的进化祖先。

[分析] 句子的主干为 he believed in a hypothesis。first put forth by Charles Darwin 是后置定语,修饰宾语。that 引导的是 hypothesis 的同位语从句。后置定语将这个同位语从句与被修饰成分分割开来,使句子呈分割结构。翻译时可将同位语顶针处理,并采用本位词和外位语的译法,添加"这个"来密切上下文逻辑关系。

此外,还有一种特殊的同位语,即同位语中包含一个定语从句的结构。我们将这种结构称为同位定语从句,翻译时采取定语从句后置的译法。

[例·真题] **It is also said he appears at the oriel window on the top floor of the house on April 23 every year—the date he is said to have been born and to have died.**

[译文] 也有人说他每年4月23日都会出现在房子顶层的凸窗旁,据说他在这天出生,也在这天逝世。

[分析] 句子的主干是 it is also said ... 。it 是形式主语,真正的主语是个主语从句 he appears at the oriel window on the top floor of the house on April 23 every year—the date he is said to have been born and to have died。在这个主语从句中,at the oriel window on the top floor of the house 是地点状语,on April 23 every year 是时间状语,the date he is said to have been born and to have died 是同位定语从句(在翻译时可后置处理,单独成句)。

7.2 插入语

插入语可以分割句子结构。它位于句中,通过标点符号与主句分割开来,可以作定语、状语和同位语。就形态而言,插入语可以是名词词组、形容词词组、副词词组、不定式结构、非谓语结构和从句。翻译时需先判断插入语在句中扮演的成分,之后将它处理成定语、状语或同位语。

[例·真题] It's hard not to wonder how subsequent events in her life—rather consequential as they have turned out to be to conservation, to science, to our sense of ourselves as a species—might have unfolded differently had someone not found her passport, along with an itinerary from Cook's, the travel agency, folded inside, and delivered it to the Cook's office.

译文 因为她生命中接下来的事迹对自然保护、科学和人类作为一个物种的自我认知都十分重要,所以人们不禁思索,如果没有人捡到她的护照及里面夹着的库克旅行社行程单,并将其送到该旅行社的话,那么这些事迹可能就要改写了。

分析 句子的主干是 it's hard。it 是形式主语,真正的主语是后面的不定式否定结构。这个不定式结构中包含一个由 how 引导的宾语从句。这个宾语从句采用了虚拟语气,其主干是 subsequent events might have unfolded。had someone not found her passport, along with an itinerary from Cook's, the travel agency, folded inside, and delivered it to the Cook's office 是条件状语从句。这句话中的插入语是一个 as 引导的原因状语从句,使用破折号与主句隔开,翻译时采取倒译的方法,将它置于句首单独成句。

[例·真题] Undergraduates will tell you that they're under pressure—from their parents, from the burden of debt they incur, from society at large—to choose majors they believe will lead as directly as possible to good jobs.

译文 本科生会告诉你,他们迫于来自父母、自己承担的债务和整个社会的压力,不得不选择他们认为可以最直接找到好工作的专业。

分析 句子的主干是 undergraduates will tell you that…。that 引导宾语从句,这个宾语从句的主干是 they're under pressure。这句话的插入语是 pressure 的后置定语,破折号将插入语与主句分割开来。不定式结构作 pressure 的后置定语,其中包含一个修饰 majors 的定语从句。翻译时,将 under pressure 这个介词短语转译为动词"迫于",插入语部分采用前置处理,定语从句成分简单,也采取前置处理的方法。

8 转 译

转译在本质上是一个润色的过程。考虑到中英差异,有时直接按照原文结构翻译会导致行文上的不通顺。因此,在英汉互译时,不能机械地将原有词性对号入座,要巧妙地运用词类转译法,使译文更符合目的语规范,表达自然地道。从单词层面看,转译主要发生在名词、动词、形容词和副词之间;从句子层面看,转译发生在各句子成分之间。

8.1 词类转换

词类转换是指在翻译过程中,为了使译文符合目的语的表达方式、方法和习惯,将原文语言中的某一词类转换成译文语言的另一种词类,是最常用、最高效的翻译方法之一。从单词层面看,词类转换主要发生在名词、动词、形容词和副词之间。

8.1.1 名转动

英语属于静态语言,较多使用名词;汉语属于动态语言,较多使用动词。在英译汉时,将英语名词转译为汉语动词能使原文信息能够准确、有效地被接收,还能使汉语译文更加流畅、地道。

[例·真题] Among foreign cultural institutes and publishers, the traditional American aversion to literature in translation is known as "the 3 percent problem".

译文 在外国文化研究所和出版社领域,美国人向来反感文学翻译作品,这就是人们常说的"3％难题"。

分析 aversion是名词,转译为同根动词"反感";to literature in translation 配合"反感"这个动词,转译为名词词组,作宾语;American是形容词,转译成名词,译为"美国人";traditional是形容词,转译为副词"向来"。

8.1.2 介转动

英文是静态的语言,常用介词结构。介词结构是英语语言的特色之一,使用范围广、频率高,含义丰富。汉语是动态的语言,常用动词结构。因此,英译汉时常常将静态的介词结构转译为汉语的动词结构。

[例·真题] Along a rugged, wide North Sea beach here on a recent day, children formed teams of 8 to 10, taking their places beside mounds of sand carefully cordoned by candy-cane striped tape.

译文 最近,孩子们沿着崎岖又广阔的北海沙滩组成了8~10人一组的团队,他们在糖果色胶带小心围起来的沙堆旁各就各位。

分析 along是介词,转译为动词"沿着",伴随状语采用顺译的方法在句尾单独成句。

8.1.3 形副转动

在英译汉时,英语中的一些形容词和副词常常根据汉语行文的需要,转译为动词。这一点在本书第5章和第6章中均有涉及,此处通过以下例子简要说明。

[例·真题] Famous because of her last name and fortune, she has always been private and publicity-averse.

译文 她因嫁入豪门、家财万贯出名,但却一向为人低调,不愿抛头露面。

分析 famous、private 和 publicity-averse 均是形容词,此处均转译为动词。其中,将 famous 转译为动词"出名",更符合汉语思维;private 和 publicity-averse 的原意分别为"私下的、私人的"和"不喜宣扬的",由于此处是对女性的评价,需考虑用词的内涵和色彩,故而译为动词词组"为人低调""不愿抛头露面",恰当准确地进行描述。

8.1.4 动转名

虽然多数情况下的英译汉是将名词转译为动词,但为了符合目的语读者的表述习惯,也可以将动词转译为名词。如果英文中的动词在翻译成中文时表述不通,则可将该动词转译为相应的名词,并根据句意增译谓语动词,形成动宾搭配。

[例·真题] Early Maori adapted the tropically based east Polynesian culture in line with the challenges associated with a larger and more diverse environment, eventually developing their own distinctive culture.

译文 早期的毛利人为应对更广阔、多元的环境所带来的挑战,对源于热带环境的东波利尼西亚文化作出调整。

分析 adapted是动词,转译为同根名词"调整",并增加译动词"对……作出",作谓语动词。

8.1.5 动转副

特别需要说明的是,在名词、动词、形容词和副词中,两两之间均可发生转译。虽然动词常常转译为名词,但是动词转译为副词的情况也是存在的。

[例·真题] There was no ordinary day at the beach, but a newly minted, state-sanctioned competition for schoolchildren to raise awareness of the dangers of rising sea levels in a country of precarious geography that has provided lessons for the world about water management, but that fears that its next generation will grow complacent.

译文 孩子们在沙滩上度过的这一天并不平凡,他们所进行的是一场新设立的由国家批准的比赛,旨在帮助学生更好地认识海平面不断上升所带来的危险。荷兰是一个地理位置险恶的国家。尽管该国在水利管理方面为世界提供样本,但是它也担心其下一代会变得自满。

分析 for schoolchildren to raise awareness 是目的状语,翻译时通过"旨在"体现逻辑关系;awareness 本是名词,转译为动词"认识";raise 是动词,转译为副词"更好地",以配合并修饰转译后的动词"认识"。

8.2 句子成分转译

我们常说的句子成分是指主语(subject)、谓语(predicate)、宾语(object)、直接宾语(direct object)、间接宾语(indirect object)、宾语补足语(object complete)、定语(attributive)、状语(adverbial)。句子成分的转译指的是把句子的某一种成分转译成另一种成分,这是翻译过程中经常使用的一种方法。

需要注意的是,句子成分的转换往往会带来连锁反应,一个句子成分发生了转换,其他成分很可能也会需要随之发生转换或变化。因此,翻译时应具体情况具体分析,努力做到译句语义完整、表述通顺。

[例·真题] "Napoleon, for these people, was very popular," Jacobs, 73, said over coffee. "That is why, still today, there are some enemies of the project."

译文 "对这些人而言,拿破仑非常受欢迎,"73岁的贾各布边喝咖啡边说,"这就是为什么直到如今仍然有人反对这个项目。"

分析 enemies 是 there be 句型的主语,是一个名词;of the project 是后置定语,修饰 enemies。翻译时,可将 enemies 转译为同根动词"反对",作 why 引导表语从句的谓语动词,并将后置定语 of the project 转译为表语从句的宾语,与转译后的谓语动词形成搭配。

9 逻 辑

中文是意合的语言,而英文是形合的语言,英汉两种语言在句法结构和用词习惯等方面都存在着显著差异。因此,英汉互译除了要斟酌表面词句的选用外,还要从整体上把握语篇的衔接和连贯。

9.1 显性的衔接

显性的衔接指的是通过词汇和语法手段明显地体现出句间的逻辑关系。英文是形合语言,多采用显性衔接。一般而言,显性衔接的手段包括照应、替代、省略和逻辑连接。

9.1.1 照应

照应指的是语篇中一个成分作为另一个成分的参照点。简而言之,照应是用代词等语法手段表示语义关系的行文方法。英语中常用代词体现形合;汉语中常省略代词体现意合。因此,英译汉往往需要省略代词,或把英语代词还原,译出其本义,抑或将代词译为"其",以密切上下文联系;汉译英为了避免重复,往往使用相应的代词来替换重复部分。

[例·真题] Her philanthropic work, especially on education causes like College Track, the college prep organization she helped found and through which she was Ms. Castro's mentor, has been her priority and focus.

译文 慈善工作是她的首要任务和重点,尤其是"大学之路"这样的教育事业。这个大学预科组织是她帮着建立的,也是在该组织,她成为了卡斯特罗的导师。

分析 本句有两个物主代词"her"和两个人称代词"she",但是汉语中通常不会频繁使用代词。全部保留这些代词既不符合汉语的行文习惯,又会造成冗余,因此删减第一个物主代词,使译文简洁流畅。

[例·真题] Despite its varied uses and renovations over the years, the 4,250-square-foot, or 395-square-meter inn has retained so much of its original character that the organization English Heritage lists it as a Grade Ⅱ property, indicating that it is particularly important and of "more than special interest".

译文 尽管这些年来这个旅馆有不同的用途,且历经多次修葺,但是这个4250平方英尺(约395平方米)的小旅馆仍然大致保留了其原始风貌,英国遗产组织将其列为国家二级文物保护单位。这表明该处遗产特别重要,具有"特别的意义"。

分析 its 和 it 均与 inn 形成照应。让步状语从句位于句首,先翻译,让步状语从句中的 its 需在翻译时应指明指代,译为"这个旅馆"而不是"它";之后与 inn 形成照应的代词则可译为"其",这样既避免了冗余,又明确了指代,不会造成歧义。

[例·真题] 在这个意义上,G20 本身就是一座桥,一座连接历史与未来、发达国家与发展中国家的桥梁。

译文 In this sense, G20 itself is a bridge, one that connects history with future, developed countries with developing ones.

分析 "一座连接历史与未来、发达国家与发展中国家的桥梁"是"桥"的同位定语从句,用 one 代替中心词"桥",与之形成照应。在定语从句中,"发达国家"和"发展中国家"均是国家,所以只保留第一个"国家",将第二个"国家"用 ones 代替。

9.1.2 替代

替代是指用简洁的语言取代语篇中的某些词语,从而避免不必要的重复。替代是一种语篇衔接手段,既避免了重复,又促进了语义衔接。替代的内容具有多样化的特点。替代分为名词性替代、动词性替代和分句替代。在英语中,替代的使用频率高于汉语。因此,英译汉常常会省略替代内容或采用重复的处理方式,汉译英则应该多用替代来衔接上下文。

[例·真题] Individual European countries and regions have banned certain genetically modified crops before. Many consumers and farmers in countries like Austria, France and Italy regard the crops as potentially dangerous and likely to contaminate organically produced food.

译文 个别欧洲国家和地区之前已经禁止了某种转基因作物。奥地利、法国与意大利这些国家的许多消费者与农户都认为转基因作物具有潜在的危险性,可能会污染有机作物。

分析 在本句中,the crops 替代了名词 genetically modified crops,译为汉语时则需要根据上下文表述逻辑重复前文中的"转基因作物"一词,把 the crops 的指代内容具体化。

[例·真题] 西藏与世界的经济联系日益密切。2012 年,全区进出口总额为 34.24 亿美元,是 1953 年 0.04 亿美元的 850 多倍,年均增长 12.1%。

译文 In terms of economy, Tibet is now more and more closely linked to the world. In 2012, the total volume of trade in this region reached 3.424 billion U.S. dollars, more than 850 times that of 1953 which was 4 million U.S. dollars, with an annual growth rate of 12.1%.

分析 这两句话中存在三处替代。"全区"代替的是前一句话中的"西藏",直接译为"this region",这样在避免重复的同时也不会造成歧义。比较结构比较的是"进出口总额",因此提到1952年西藏的进出口总额时,将"进出口总额"用"that"代替,并用定语从句引出1952年西藏进出口总额的具体数值,定语从句的关系代词"which"代替了1952年西藏的进出口总额。

9.1.3 省略

省略是为了避免重复,突出新信息和行文连接的一种语法手段。省略分为名词性省略、动词性省略和分句省略。对带有省略信息的英文句子,英译汉应根据上下文将省略信息进行适当地填补或舍弃,从而增强译文的流畅度和逻辑性。

[例·真题] While some people said Ms. Powell Jobs should have started a foundation in Mr. Jobs's name after his death, she did not, nor has she increased her public giving.

译文 尽管有人说鲍威尔·乔布斯女士本应在乔布斯逝世后以乔布斯的名义成立一个基金会,但她并没有这样做,也没有增加公共捐赠。

分析 she did not 的后面省略了 start a foundation in Mr. Jobs's name after his death,是动词性省略。省略后的英语句子简洁直接,在英译汉时,例句中的省略信息不影响汉语的表达,因此我们也可将省略信息进行舍弃,使译文变得更简洁。

9.1.4 逻辑连接

逻辑连接词是连接并表现句子间逻辑关系的词语。汉语中的"并且""但是""因为……所以……"或英语中的 and、but、because 等词语都是逻辑连接词。这些词语是语句逻辑的形式符号,是显性连接。

[例·真题] Although there are significant hurdles, geologists say that the Vaca Muerta is a harbinger of a possible major expansion of global petroleum supplies over the next two decades as the industry uses advanced techniques to extract oil from shale and other tightly packed rocks.

译文 虽然存在重大障碍,但是地质学家称,因为该行业运用先进技术从页岩和其他致密岩石中提取石油,所以瓦卡穆尔塔预示着未来20年全球天然气供应将大幅增加。

分析 在这句话中,各层的逻辑关系是显性的。although 引导的是让步状语从句,体现转折关系,翻译时通过"虽然"表现出这层逻辑关系;as 引导的是原因状语从句,体现因果关系,翻译时通过"因为"表现出这层逻辑关系。

9.2 隐性的连贯

连贯(coherence)指的是意义和概念之间隐性的连接手段,主要体现在语义层面上。汉语是意合的语言,多采用隐性的连贯。连贯主要体现在三个层面上,即词汇、句法和语境。

9.2.1 词汇连贯

词汇引导的连贯往往可以构成隐性的连贯,主要通过词汇复现和词汇同现的关系来实现。词汇复现指的是通过词语的重复、近义词或概括词等来构成语篇的连贯性和完整性。词汇同现指的是词汇共同出现的倾向性。在语篇中,围绕一定的话题,一定的词往往会同时出现。因此,英汉翻译需要在选词上保持一致性。

[例·真题] New Zealand music has been influenced by blues, jazz, country, rock and roll, and hip hop, with many of these genres given a unique New Zealand interpretation. Maori developed traditional chants and songs from their ancient South-East Asian origins, and after centuries of isolation created a unique "monotonous" and "doleful" sound.

译文 新西兰音乐受布鲁斯、爵士、乡村、摇滚和嘻哈音乐的影响,很多音乐类别都带有独特的新西兰元素。毛利人以古东南亚为基,形成了自己的吟唱传统,在与世隔绝数百年后,创造了"单调"和"忧伤"的独特曲调。

分析 在本句中,music、blues、jazz、country、rock and roll、hip hop、genres、chants and songs 和 sound 都与音乐有关,彼此间具有用词上的一致性和连贯性。因此,英译汉也应做到这一点,如:blues 译为"布鲁斯"而非"忧郁",country 译为"乡村"而非"国家"或"乡下",chants and songs 译为"吟唱"而非"圣歌"或"歌词",sound 译为"曲调"而非"声音"。

[例·真题] Dating from 1534, the inn, now called Shakespeare House, is thought to have been built as a Tudor hunting lodge. Later it became a stop for travelers between London and Stratford-upon-Avon, where Shakespeare was born and buried.

译文 这家旅馆始建于1534年,现在被称作"莎士比亚故居"。有人认为该旅馆最初是都铎王朝时期的狩猎旅馆,后来成为往返伦敦和斯特拉特福的旅客在中途歇脚的地方。斯特拉特福是莎士比亚的出生地,也是他的安葬地。

分析 the inn、lodge、it 以及 a stop 指的均是同一建筑。因为英文不喜重复用词,所以后文中均采用了"the inn"的近义词。汉语常常会重复用同一个词,所以翻译时统一翻译成"旅馆"。

9.2.2 句法连贯

从句法结构层面看,汉语多流水小句,句间逻辑通过句意隐晦地体现出来。因此,汉译英需要厘清句子内部及句子与句子之间的逻辑关系,然后将这一关系用逻辑连词、非谓语结构或不定式结构等表现出来。

[例·真题] 矿产资源是人类生存和社会发展的重要物质基础,加快矿产资源的开发利用,发挥矿产资源勘探的潜力作用。

译文 Mineral resources are a significant physical foundation for human survival and social development. As a result, these resources should be exploited at a faster pace and their potential should be realized.

<u>分析</u> 本句话由三个流水小句组成，看似并列，实则前一句话与后两句话之间呈隐性的因果逻辑关系，翻译时通过 as a result 将隐性的因果关系表现出来。

9.2.3 语境连贯

一般而言，英语中的语境指的是语言环境中的上下文，又指使话语得以进行，文句赖以存在的情境。而语体是语言的功能变体。一个人说话时的情景，包括说话的内容、对象、场合以及说话的目的和动机都可能影响语体的使用。

[例·真题] Everyone knows that weddings—the most elaborate and costly form of old school pageantry still acceptable in modern society—are stupid expensive.

<u>译文</u> 众所周知，婚礼如此昂贵实在毫无意义，可当今社会仍然沿袭对婚事大操大办的传统。

<u>分析</u> 本句包含了一个同位语，即 the most elaborate and costly form of old school pageantry still acceptable in modern society，其作用是对 wedding 进行解释说明。这里需要将 modern society 译为主语"当今社会"，acceptable 转译为动词"沿袭"，the most elaborate and costly form of old school pageantry 译为"对婚事大操大办的传统"。并且，由于原句中的同位语成分与主句呈转折逻辑关系，在语篇上来说，需要变换位置，放到最后译，可以让中文更加顺畅。该文主要反映了当代美国人婚礼消费过高的问题。这篇杂志文章的用词较口语化，语言幽默风趣，讽刺了当时非理性的婚庆消费现象。因此在翻译时，也要运用口语化的表达来保留原文的语体风格。

英语句子常见复合长句，因而英译汉时应首先理顺语句间逻辑关系，然后在此基础上对语义进行合理分析并译为多个汉语小句，必要时应增加适当的连接词，以保证句法上的连贯。

[例·真题] Many people industry and the sevices, who have pratical experience of noise, regard any investigation of this question as a waste of time; they are not prepared even to admit the possibility that noise affects people.

<u>译文</u> 很多在工业部门工作，或是去部队服役的人，他们对噪声有切身的体会，但是这些人却认为，噪声问题的研究纯属浪费时间，他们甚至不愿意承认噪声对人体有任何影响。

<u>分析</u> who 引导的主语从句修饰主语 many people，它和主句之间有逻辑关系，构成转折。这点在翻译时需体现出来，以使句法衔接紧凑。

10　长　句

英语长句一般是由于修饰成分（如介词短语、不定式短语及从句等）、并列成分过多，或是句式结构过于复杂导致的，且英语句子呈树状结构，在主干的基础上根据语法规则展开。因此，在翻译英语长句时可以先找出句子的主干成分和修饰成分，然后进行句型解析，再进一步润色得出译文。在一般情况下，英语长句的翻译可以有三种处理方式：单独处理分译法、意合综合法和习惯顺逆法。

10.1　单独处理分译法

在翻译长句时，可将原句中的某个成分或分句拆分出来进行单独处理，从而让译文逻辑清晰、层次分明。并列成分或修饰部分过长时通常采用分译法进行处理。

[例·真题] Mr. Raby said: "The size of the find gives us a sense of two things: a sense of China as a country already producing things on an industrialized scale and also a China that is no longer producing ceramics to bury."

译文　雷比先生说："本次大规模的发现说明了两件事：一是中国当时已经开始进行规模化生产；二是中国生产的瓷器不再用于陪葬。"

分析　首先提取主干和修饰部分。这句直接引语的主干：the size of the find gives us a sense of two things。修饰部分：同位语①a sense of China as a country already producing things on an industrialized scale，②a China that...。其次进行句型解析。同位语间的逻辑关系为并列关系。由于句子较长，同位语可处理为主谓句。

10.2　意合综合法

意合综合法是指在充分理解原文的基础上，调整原文句子的结构和顺序，重新组合原句中的信息。它应用到翻译过程中，即将英文这类形合语言转变为汉语这类意合语言，在传达原文的主要信息时，做到语义完整、符合逻辑、句式整齐。

[例·真题] Despite that far-flung status, Madeira catapulted into the center of the Union's agricultural and environmental affairs last year when Portugal asked the European Commission for permission to impose an unprecedented ban on growing biotech crops there.

译文 去年葡萄牙向欧盟委员会提出申请,要在马德拉群岛实施一项前所未有的禁令,即禁止当地种植转基因作物。这让原本远离欧洲大陆的马德拉群岛迅速成为了欧盟农业和环境问题的焦点。

分析 首先提取句子主干和修饰部分。句子的主干:Madeira catapulted into the center。修饰部分:让步状语,despite that far-flung status;时间状语从句,last year when Portugal asked…。其次进行句型解析。让步状语的处理:定语与状语互换,可译为定语。时间状语从句的处理:当句子中有从句出现时,需要调整句子结构和句子顺序,优先翻译从句。主从逻辑关系为因果关系。

10.3 习惯顺逆法

习惯顺逆法即顺序法和逆序法,在翻译中较为常见。当英文长句的逻辑顺序与汉语表达基本一致时,可采用顺序法按照原句语序进行翻译。如果英文长句的逻辑顺序与汉语表达相反,则需要采用逆序法,将原句顺序反过来进行翻译。

10.3.1 顺序法

[例·真题] One of the current owners, Nick Underwood, said the local lore goes even further, "it is also said he appears at the oriel window on the top floor of the house on April 23 every year—the date he is said to have been born and to have died."

译文 房屋所有人之一的尼克·安德伍德说当地有关这座房屋的传说更是神乎其神:"莎士比亚每年4月23日都会出现在顶楼的凸窗前,据说那天既是他的生日,也是他的忌日。"

分析 在这句话中,各个句子成分的排列顺序和表意方式与汉语基本一致,故可以采取顺序法进行翻译。

10.3.2 逆序法

[例·真题] That has left Madeira with "much the largest extent of laurel forest surviving in the world, with a unique suite of plants and animals", according to the United Nations Educational, Scientific and Cultural Organization, which named the Madeiran laurisilva a World Heritage Site in 1999.

译文 联合国教科文组织于1999年将马德拉月桂树列入《世界遗产名录》,并称马德拉拥有世界上现存最大的月桂林,林中还生活着许多独有的动植物。

分析 由于这句话中评注性状语部分的修饰成分过多,翻译时放在后面容易导致句子前后不均,加之按照中文表达习惯,应先说状语部分。故在翻译时采用逆序法。

11　词和表达的选择

在翻译实践中，英语和汉语并不总是一一对应的，有时可能出现一对多或没有对应词或对应表达的现象。因此，译者需要仔细推敲、斟酌选词、准确表达。

11.1　词

通常而言，一个英文单词在不同的语境下有不同的含义。所以，需根据语境中词义的广狭、褒贬、语体、文化内涵来选择合适的单词。

11.1.1　广义与狭义

许多词汇根据上下文语境的不同，其词义的广狭也会有所改变，因此，翻译时需要结合具体的语境来区分词汇的广义、狭义。

[例·真题] Scientists analyzing data from a NASA spacecraft have found the first evidence that briny water flowed on the surface of Mars as recently as last summer, a paper published on Monday showed, raising the possibility that the planet could support <u>life</u>.

译文　周一发表的一份论文表明，分析美国国家航空航天局（NASA）飞船数据的科学家已经找到了首个证据证明去年夏天就有盐水流经火星表面，这一发现增加了火星可以维持<u>生命</u>的可能性。

分析　名词 life 在此处意为"生命"。

[例·真题] Today, bar codes appear on the surface of almost every product of contemporary <u>life</u>.

译文　在当代<u>生活</u>中，几乎所有商品的包装上都有条形码。

分析　名词 life 在此处意为"生活"。

11.1.2　贬义与褒义

词汇常常带有贬义或褒义的感情色彩，而选择带有何种感情色彩的词语由上下文语境以及原作者的观点态度决定。

[例·真题] While <u>full-blown</u> narcissists often report high levels of personal satisfaction, they create havoc and misery around them.

译文 尽管严重的自恋者常高度自满,但他们会给周围人带来灾难和痛苦。

分析 "full-blown"原意为"成熟的,全面的",此处用来形容自恋者,且后文提到了其危害,故而译为偏贬义的"严重的",使它更符合原文感情色彩。

[例·真题] He holed up at his grandparents' home in Miami Beach, where he spent the winter of 1948—1949 in a chair in the sand, thinking.

译文 1948年到1949年的那个冬天,他在迈阿密海滩的祖父母家里闭关,坐在沙滩的椅子上冥思苦想。

分析 hole up原意为"躲藏在",此处原文指的是主角为了破解难题,远离世人独自专心思考,故而译为偏褒义的"闭关",使其更符合原文感情色彩。

11.1.3 语体

英文文章的语体风格多种多样,或口语化,或正式,或幽默讽刺,抑或专业正式。因此,在翻译过程中,需选择语体风格与文章总体风格相似的词语。

[例·真题] But it turns out Americans are now blowing even more money than ever before on what's supposed to be the most magic day of any couple's life together.

译文 不过,如今美国人结起婚来比过去更烧钱,因为大家都将婚礼当天视为夫妻共同生活中最美妙的日子。

分析 该句截取于一篇杂志文章,主要反映了当代美国人婚礼消费过高的问题。这篇杂志文章,其用词较口语化,语言幽默风趣,讽刺了当时非理性的婚庆消费现象。因此在选词时,也要运用口语化词汇来保留原文的语体风格,将blow money译为"烧钱"。

[例·真题] Despite that far-flung status, Madeira catapulted into the center of the Union's agricultural and environmental affairs last year when Portugal asked the European Commission for permission to impose an unprecedented ban on growing biotech crops there.

译文 尽管马德拉群岛与欧洲大陆相隔甚远,但去年葡萄牙向欧盟委员会提出申请,要在马德拉群岛实施一项前所未有的禁令,禁止当地种植转基因作物,此举使得马德拉群岛迅速成为欧盟农业和环境问题的焦点。

分析 该句语体类似于国际政治新闻,因此译文用词必须严谨正式,才能体现原文的语气语体特点。所以,将far-flung status译为四字格"相隔甚远";将ask...for permission译为"向……提出申请"。

11.1.4 文化内涵

语言承载着文化,不同的语言有不同的文化内涵和本文化专属的习语。因此,需首先了解习语的内涵,再根据上下文语境选出最能传达该词本意的目的语词汇或短语。

[例·真题] The runaway success of Stieg Larsson's *Millennium* trilogy suggests that when it comes to contemporary literature in translation, Americans are at least willing to read Scandinavian detective fiction.

译文 斯蒂格·拉森(Steig Larsson)的《千禧年》三部曲迅速走红，这表明，当谈到现代文学翻译作品时，美国人至少还愿意阅读斯堪的纳维亚的侦探小说。

分析 在本句中，runaway success 是英语习语，不能直接译为"失控的成功"，应译为"迅速走红"或"一炮而红"，才能语言精练，表意准确。

11.2 表 达

为了使译文更符合目的语读者的语言习惯，翻译时可采取正反表达转换的方法处理译文。正反表达转换包括正话反说和反话正说。

11.2.1 正话反说

正话反说指的是把原文中的肯定说法转换为译文中的否定说法。

英语中带有"否认、拒绝、抑制、禁止、阻碍"等意义的词虽然形式上看似肯定，但意义上却属于否定的范围。这类意义否定的词包括：动词，如 prevent、fail、miss、deny、refuse、avoid、forbid 等；名词，如 loss、neglect、ignorance、vain、shortage 等；形容词，如 bad、short、ignorant、absent、last 等；介词，如 beyond、except、above、beneath、past 等。英译汉时需将这些看似肯定的表达转换成否定的说法，使其更符合汉语的表达习惯。

[例·真题] City Hall refers to the project as "eco-grazing", and it notes that the four ewes will prevent the use of noisy, gas-guzzling mowers and cut down on the use of herbicides.

译文 市政厅把该项目称为"生态割草"，并指出，引进这四只母羊后，就无需使用噪声大、耗油多的割草机了，也减少了除草剂的使用。

分析 在本句中，prevent 虽在内容上是否定的，但在形式上却是肯定的。如果将其译为"阻止(使用)……"，则不符合中文的语言习惯，容易造成"翻译腔"。处理这类"形式上肯定，但意义上否定"的动词、名词、形容词、介词等词类时，需要采用"正话反说"的处理方法。

英语中有些动词短语或介词短语也含有否定的含义，比如动词短语 protect...from、keep...from、restrain...from 等，形容词短语 free from、lack of、short of 等，介词短语 out of question、far from、anything but、at a loss、instead of 等。在英汉互译时，这些肯定形式的短语也可以转换为否定形式。

[例·真题] Perhaps the best part of being free from the shackles of wedding planning is the opportunity to treat yourself.

译文 或许，不受婚礼计划束缚的最大好处就是有机会善待自己。

分析 在本句中，be free from 原意为"从……中脱离"，通过"正话反说"的方法处理之后，译为"不受"，这样不仅使句子的表达更通顺，而且更符合中文的逻辑习惯。

此外，英语中也有类似 would rather、unless、but for、more of...than、too...to 等的结构。这些结构虽然在形式上是肯定的，但在意义上可能含有虚拟、让步、转折等否定含义，翻译时也需要转换为汉语的否定结构。

[例·真题] It's more of a set of progressive symptoms (like alcoholism) than an identifiable state (like diabetes).

译文 它与其说是一系列逐渐严重的症状（如酗酒），不如说是某种可以识别的症状（如糖尿病）。

分析 上述例子中的固定结构 more of...than 虽然在形式上是肯定的，但在翻译时需转换成中文里的否定结构，译为"与其说……不如说……"。

英语中有些句子的肯定表达是为了使语气缓和，传达委婉的含义或者表示礼貌，这种情况下原文的肯定形式也要转换为否定形式，从而使句意更符合交际习惯。

[例·真题] Fossil charcoals tell us that wildfires have been part of life on Earth for as long as there have been plants on land.

译文 木炭化石表明，野火一直是地球上的一部分，其历史并不比植物出现在陆地上的时间短。

分析 上述例子中，为强调野火在地球上存在时间之长，采用了 as long as 这个比较结构，将其与植物在陆地上的时间作对比。翻译时采用正话反说的方法，将比较结构译为"并不比……短"。

11.2.2 反话正说

反话正说指的是把原文中的否定说法转换为译文中的肯定说法。

英文中的否定词 not、no、never、seldom、hardly 等，或带有如 dis-、il-、un-、in-、im-、non-、-less 等否定词缀的词语或词组，以及像 no/not...until、can't be 这样的否定结构，尽管含义上是否定的，但在翻译时也可以转换为肯定形式。

[例·真题] It's notable for occasions like Valentine's Day that narcissists struggle to stay committed to romantic partners, in no small part because they find themselves superior.

译文 在情人节等时候，自恋症患者明显会在忠诚于恋人的问题上挣扎一番，这在很大程度上是因为他们觉得自己高人一等。

分析 in no small part 本意是"在不小的程度上"，为否定表达，且不符合中文表达习惯。因此反话正说，将其译为"在很大程度上"。

[例·真题] Ancient records told of Persian fleets sailing the Southeast Asian seas but <u>no wrecks had been found</u>, <u>until</u> the Belitung dhow.

译文 古记录表明，曾有波斯舰队航行到东南亚海域，但<u>直到</u>发现勿里洞岛三角帆船时，<u>才</u>找到一些残骸。

分析 为使行文顺畅，将 no ... until 的结构反话正说，处理为"直到……才（找到一些残骸）"，而不是"没有（残骸被找到），直到……"。

12 被动语态

英汉两种语言差异较大,尤其体现在被动语态上。英语被动语态广泛用于新闻报道、科技和学术论文等文体,强调所叙述的事物本身,更加客观、正式。被动语态在汉语中的使用频率较低,因此英译汉时常采用变主动或换说法的方法处理被动语态,使其更符合汉语表达习惯。

12.1 变主动

英文中的被动语态可以转换成中文中的主动语态。"被动变主动"主要有以下四种方法。

第一种方法是不改变主语及句子结构,直接转换成主动语态。因为汉语里表示被动意义的句子可以不用"被"字而直接采用主动形态的形式,所以英译汉时可直接省略"被"字,却不改变句子结构。

[例·真题] Its Dutch-speaking regions were part of the Kingdom of the Netherlands, while the French-speaking portion had been incorporated into the French Empire.

译文 其荷兰语区是荷兰王国的一部分,而法语区则归并入法兰西帝国。

分析 had been incorporated into 是被动结构,如果保留被动,则译为"被归并入……",这并不符合汉语的表达习惯。而省略"被"字并不影响中文语义表达,所以翻译时在原文顺序的基础上只需省略"被"字。

[例·真题] Increasingly, that campaign is no longer limited to widely spoken language like French and German.

译文 该活动渐渐不再局限于法语和德语等广泛使用的语言。

分析 is no longer limited to 是被动结构,原意为"不再被局限于……",如此翻译并不符合汉语表达习惯,因此不用"被"字,译为"不再局限于……"。

第二种方法是根据句意将原句的其他成分译为汉语的主语。当 by、in 等介词引导的状语是谓语动词动作的发出者时,常用这种方法将状语转译为主语,并适当添加"把""给"等弱动词,从而使句子变成主动句。

[例·真题] In the 20th century, it was owned by two American families.

译文 两个美国家庭于 20 世纪拥有了这处房产。

分析 by 引导的方式状语是谓语动词动作的发出者,将其作为主语,转换成主动句,并结合上下文具体指出 it 指代的东西。

[例·真题] The pesticide was banned this year for use on many flowering crops in Europe that attract honey bees.

译文 今年欧洲已禁止对许多吸引蜜蜂的开花作物使用该杀虫剂。

分析 in 引导的地点状语是谓语动词动作的发出者,将其作为主语,并将原句的主语转译为谓语动词的宾语加以配合,以实现"被动变主动"。

第三种"变主动"的情况是,当保留英语被动句的主语会造成语义不通,句中的其他成分也很难译为主语时,可以添加"人们""我们""有人""大家"等泛指代词作主语。

[例·真题] For more than a decade, archaeologists and historians have been studying the contents of a ninth-century Arab dhow that was discovered in 1998 off Indonesia's Belitung Island.

译文 十多年来,考古学家和历史学家一直在研究一艘九世纪阿拉伯三角帆船的内容物,这艘三角帆船是人们于 1998 年在印度尼西亚勿里洞岛附近发现的。

分析 be discovered 这个被动语态若是直接译为"被发现"则不符合中文的表达习惯,且句中并无可作"discovered"逻辑主语的成分,因此添加泛指代词"人们",将定语从句部分"被动变主动"。

[例·真题] A rambling though dilapidated farmstead called Hougoumont, which was crucial to the battle's outcome, is being painstakingly restored as an educational center.

译文 霍高蒙特(Hougoumont)对此次战役的胜败举足轻重,如今人们正煞费苦心地将这座广袤而破败的农庄修复成一座教育中心。

分析 be restored 意为"被修复",不符合中文表达习惯,且该句中没有可以作 restored 逻辑主语的成分,所以添加泛指代词"人们",从而避免被动的说法,使译文更符合中文习惯。

第四种方法是将英文被动句译为汉语无主句。英汉的一大差异在于,英语必须有主语,而汉语可以没有主语。因此,如果英文被动句中的主语或其他成分不宜译作汉语主动句中的主语,而加译一个主语又无必要,那么可以将句子翻译成汉语的无主句,尤其是表示建议、命令、请求、要求的句子。

[例·真题] Core samples need to be retrieved from thousands of feet below the surface to judge how much oil or gas can be retrieved.

译文 并且,还需从地表下数千英尺处提取核心样本以判断可提取多少油气。

分析 中文描述步骤常用无主句式。因此,先翻译被动语态的谓语动词,再翻译被动语态的逻辑宾语,即句子主语,使之成为一个主动的无主句。

[例·真题] That data was then correlated with high-resolution images of the streaks.

译文 之后,将那份数据与纹路沟壑的高分辨率成像进行比对。

分析 本句话是科技文体中常常出现的描述步骤的句子,可译为汉语无主句,保留原句谓语动词,并把原句主语转译为谓语动词的宾语。

12.2 换说法

英语被动句译为中文时也可保留被动,但需要换说法。一般而言,可将"被"的说法换成"为……所……""是由……""受……""可以……"等。

[例·真题] But the archivists have had to be trained to care for the animals.

译文 但是,为了照顾这些动物,档案管理员不得不接受了训练。

分析 本句话的译文保留了原文的语序和被动 be trained,但为了符合汉语表达习惯,将"被训练"这个说法转换成了"受到了训练"。

[例·真题] Scientists suspected the streaks were cut by flowing water, but had previously been unable to make the measurements.

译文 科学家们怀疑这些沟槽是由水流冲刷而成的,但他们之前一直无法对这些沟槽进行测量。

分析 本句话中的被动结构 be cut by flowing water 在英译汉时转换了说法,译为"是由……"的结构,即"是由水流冲刷而成的"。

[例·真题] The soulful connection with another person, the enjoyment of a beautiful hike alone, or a prayer of thanks over your sleeping child could be considered expressions of self-love.

译文 与其他人有共鸣,喜欢独自徒步欣赏美景,抑或是看着自己熟睡的孩子感恩祷告,这些都可以视作自爱的表现形式。

分析 本句话中有一个被动结构 be considered,在翻译时可转换为"可以……"的句式,即"可以视作……"。

13 增　减

增减即翻译过程中的增译和省译现象,本质上是由中英文的不同语言特征导致的。英文中常常增添代词或是省略部分词意,不会影响整体句意,但翻译成中文时,往往会出现句意不通的现象。此时,为更准确地表达原文意思,译者就要考虑在词汇和句法结构上增加或减少相应部分,主要表现在对动词、范畴词、代词或连词等的处理上。

13.1 动　词

中文为动态语言,善用动词;而英文为静态语言,善用名词和介词短语。因此,英译汉往往会出现增译动词的现象。这种现象主要分为两种情况。一种是自然增词,因为宾语缺少与之搭配的动词,所以为符合中文表达习惯,需要增加动词;另一种则是人为增词,比如抽象名词,在翻译时可能需要增加动词。

[例·真题] It generates the lessons, the tests and it grades the tests.

译文 这款软件可以上课、出试卷,还可以进行打分。

分析 这句话中存在典型的自然增词现象。generates 与两个名词宾语 lessons、tests 相搭配,在翻译时,就需要根据中文的语言习惯增加动词,使每个宾语都有动词与之相配,即"上课""出试卷"。

[例·真题] Each day, School of One software generated individualized math "playlist" for students who then chose the "modality" in which they wished to learn—software, a virtual teacher or a flesh-and-blood one.

译文 "个人学校"软件每天都为学生打造个性化的"播放列表",之后由学生们自愿选择上课方式,包括软件授课、虚拟教师授课或者真人教师授课。

分析 在这句话中,名词 software、a virtual teacher、a flesh-and-blood one 前没有动词,但按照汉语的语言习惯,在叙述时往往增加动词,从而与名词形成搭配。这里增加了"授课"这一动词词组,组成了"用软件授课"这一动宾搭配。

[例·真题] This denial, which is contrary to the letter and spirit of the law, is being appealed.

译文 申请遭拒既违背了法律的条文,又违背了法律所具有的精神,现该基金会正据此提出上诉。

分析 在这句话中,spirit 作为抽象名词,且本身没有动词词根,在翻译时为更加符合汉语表达习惯,增译了动词"具有",属于人为增词现象。

13.2 范畴词

范畴词包括问题、状态、情况、工作等,其本身并没有实际意义,在英文中往往不会体现出来,但由于中文的语言习惯,翻译时需要增添相应的范畴词,从而使译文更加通顺、合理。

[例·真题] Aggregates hide inequality.

译文 经济总量会掩盖不平等问题。

分析 在这句话中,如果直接翻译出来则是"经济总量掩盖不平等",不符合中文的表达习惯,故而选择了增加范畴词"问题",从而让译文更加通畅。

13.3 代词连词

13.3.1 增减代词

英文中多用代词,而中文中通常不会多次重复使用代词,英译汉时全部保留英文原文中的代词会使译文冗长,故翻译时需要灵活删减代词。比如:含有泛指意义的人称代词 we、you 和不定代词 one 等作主语时,以及 it 作非人称主语或形式主语、形式宾语时,通常可以省略不译。此外,英文中还会出现为起到照应作用而使用的代词 his、our、their 等,也可以作省译处理,从而使译文的语篇衔接更为顺畅。

[例·真题] Second, we also need increased financial inclusion.

译文 第二,提高金融包容性。

[例·真题] Mayor Bertrand Delanoë has made the environment a priority since his election in 2001.

译文 勃兰特·狄兰诺(Bertrand Delanoë)自 2001 年当选为巴黎市长以来就将环境问题列为重中之重。

分析 在这句话中,物主代词 his 如果直译,则从句为"自从 2001 年他的选举以来",不符合中文的表达习惯,句意也不通顺,所以需要采取省代词的方法,不翻译 his,而是与主语结合起来,最终得到上述译文。

除此之外,在英译汉过程中,为使行文简洁,同时让语篇衔接顺畅,通常会增加代词"其"来替代或指代上文中的内容,衔接上下文。

[例·真题] "The importance of this discovery goes well beyond the volume," said Sebastián Eskenazi, YPF's chief executive, as he announced the find. "The important thing is it is something new: new energy, a new future, new expectations."

译文 YPF 公司首席执行官塞巴斯蒂安·埃斯肯纳齐在宣布这一重大发现时说:"这一发现的重大意义不仅仅在于油田储量巨大,还在于其全'新'性:新能源、新未来、新期待。"

分析 在这句话中,原文中两次提到 the importance,如果在翻译时全部译出会使译文冗余,故可以增加代词"其"来替代 the important thing,从而让译文的语篇结构更为简洁、清晰,也更贴合中文的表达习惯。

13.3.2 增减连词

英语作为形合语言,多用连词连接各个分句;而汉语作为意合语言,往往会隐含一些逻辑关系。英译汉时应根据语意适当地减少连词。

[例·真题] Like charges repel each other while opposite charges attract.

译文 电荷同性相斥,异性相吸。

分析 此外,值得注意的是,英文主句与从句之间通常会存在逻辑关系,在翻译成中文时,需要理清其逻辑,根据语境增加相应的逻辑连词。

[例·真题] "Scientific" creationism, which is being pushed by some for "equal time" in the classrooms whenever the scientific accounts of evolution are given, is based on religion, not science.

译文 "科学"造物论是基于宗教,而非科学。但是每当讲授进化论的科学时,一些人就推动造物论在课堂上的"同等学时"。

分析 这句话中并没有出现明显的逻辑连词,但是英文中一旦出现从句,我们就要注意观察从句和主句之间是否存在逻辑关系。这句话中主句和从句之间为转折关系,所以在翻译时要增加逻辑连词"但是"。

通过这一章的学习,我们发现增减现象的出现基本都是基于英汉语言习惯的不同。在翻译过程中,译者应当根据实际情况,灵活地对各个成分进行增减,以满足不同语言表达习惯的需要。

14 数　　词

英汉对数字的表达也有着明显的差异,处理方式主要分为两种。一种是基本直译,大都不需要变化太多句式结构,只需将原文数字表意准确译出即可,如倍数、分数和百分比等;另一种则是数词的虚指现象,翻译时需结合上下文语境和中英文表达习惯进行相应的归化异化处理。

14.1　倍数的翻译

在英译汉过程中,分数或百分数的翻译形式较为单一,而倍数的翻译会稍显复杂。倍数的英文表达常见三种形式,即"倍数词＋as＋形容词/副词＋as""倍数词＋形容词/副词比较级＋than"和"倍数词＋名词(the size/length/width/height/age 等)＋of"。

在翻译过程中,有两点需要注意。一是分清楚是增加的倍数还是减少的百分数:以增加为例,如果倍数后面接的是 as much as,意思是前者是后者的 x 倍;如果接了 more than,则表示前者比后者多 x 倍,或是增长了 $x+1$ 倍。二是遇到减少时,翻译过程中需要注意汉语的表达习惯,一般不采用"减少/减少到 x 倍"的说法,而是采用"减少了/减少到几分之几"的说法。

14.1.1　倍数词＋as＋形容词/副词＋as

[例·真题] The melting surface darkens, absorbing up to four times as much as energy from the sun as snow, which reflects sunlight.

译文　冰融化后表面变暗,吸收的太阳热量是雪的 4 倍之多,因为雪会反射太阳光。

[例·真题] The hydrogen atom is nearly 16 times as light as the oxygen atom.

译文　氢原子的质量约为氧原子的 1/16(即比氧原子约轻 15/16)。

分析　在这种形式中,倍数词也可以置于"as...as"结构之后。

[例·真题] As global climate change threatens to raise sea levels by as much as four feet by the end of the century...

译文　海平面受全球气候变暖影响,截至本世纪末可能会上涨 4 英尺之多……

14.1.2　倍数词＋形容词/副词比较级＋than

[例] His income is 3 times less than hers.

译文　他的收入是她的三分之一。

14.1.3　倍数词＋名词(the size/length/width/height/age 等)＋of

[例·真题] Experts say this is the clearest sign that India will fail to meet the goal set by the education minister, who has pledged to more than double the size of the country's higher education system by 2020.

[译文] 印度教育部部长曾表示到2020年要将印度高等教育体系的规模至少翻一番，但专家们称师资缺编问题清楚地说明印度将无法实现这一目标。

14.2　数词的归化与异化

汉语的数词有实指和虚指两种功能。实指的数词应从实在的数目上去理解，而虚指的数词则不能拘泥于实在的数字，否则便无法准确地传递原文的意思和情感。比如，文言文中常用数字"三"和"九"泛指很多、数量大："三思而行"指经过反复考虑然后再做，而不是说只思考三次；"九死一生"形容处在生死关头，情况十分危急，而不是指九成概率死，一成概率生。在英语中也是如此，某些数字往往不表示字面上具体数字的实际概念，而表示一种虚指，可以是说话人一种夸张的表达方式，也可以引申为某种抽象、比喻的意义。

由于中英文中都会存在特殊的数词虚指现象，故而这类数词在翻译时则需要综合考虑上下文语境和语言文化意义等方面，通过归化异化等翻译策略进行处理，从而准确传达句意。

[例·真题] I just became 10 times more appreciative of her humility and how humble she was in working with us in East Palo Alto.

[译文] 我极为钦佩她那种谦逊的态度以及她与我们一道在帕洛阿尔托工作时所显示出的那种谦虚精神。

[分析] 在这句话中，10 times 显然是虚指，如果将其直译为"我10倍地欣赏她谦逊的态度"，会造成词不达意。在这里，10 times 表示泛指，即非常多、极其，故可译为"极为敬佩"。

[例·真题] Two heads are better than one.

[译文] 三个臭皮匠胜过诸葛亮。

[分析] 这句话是中英文中非常典型的俗语。虽然中英文表达上存在很多差异，但仍有很多俗语、谚语在语意和语言形式上非常相近，此时可以采用归化策略，追求句子内涵的传达，从而更贴合目的语读者的语言习惯。

[例] One apple a day keeps the doctor away.

[译文] 一天一个苹果，医生远离我。

[分析] 这句话是非常常见的英文谚语，考虑到汉语中没有特别贴合的对应表达，故可以采用异化的翻译策略，直接将原文中的数词进行直译，这样既不会产生语意偏差，也可以很好地保留原句中的数字意象和文化内涵。

15 专有名词

专有名词指的是人名、地名、机构名、活动组织名、报纸杂志图书名以及影视作品名称等。翻译这些专有名词时,应遵循约定俗成的译法;而对于译名不固定的专有名词,应按照音译等翻译方法进行处理。

15.1 人名与地名

英语中无固定译文的人名、地名常以目的语国家地区的通用标准发音为依据,采用音译法翻译。当然,也可以回译已被译为目的语的人名、地名。

[例·真题] Norman Joseph Woodland was born in Atlantic City on Sept. 6, 1921.

译文 诺曼·约瑟夫·伍德兰于 1921 年 9 月 6 日出生在大西洋城。

分析 Norman Joseph Woodland 是无固定译法的人名,音译为"诺曼·约瑟夫·伍德兰";Atlantic City 是美国的一个城市,有固定译法,因而遵循固定译法译为"大西洋城"。

15.2 组织机构和活动名称

一般而言,组织机构和活动名称遵循约定俗成的固定译法,或采取直译的方法处理。

[例·真题] The Hirshhorn Museum and Sculpture Garden in Washington prohibited the sticks this month, and the Museum of Fine Arts in Houston plans to impose a ban.

译文 本月华盛顿的赫施霍恩博物馆和雕塑园开始实施自拍杆禁令,位于休斯敦的美术馆也计划发布禁令。

分析 the Hirshhorn Museum 遵循固定译法,译为"赫施霍恩博物馆";Sculpture Garden 以及 the Museum of Fine Arts 分别直译为"雕塑园"和"美术馆";Washington 和 Houston 是有固定译法的地名,译为"华盛顿"和"休斯顿"。

但是,有些组织机构和活动名称的字面意思在上下文语境中并不成立,这时需要采取意译的方法进行处理。

[例·真题] Scientists suspected the streaks, known as recurring slope lineae, or RSL, were cut by flowing water, but previously had been unable to make the measurements.

译文 这些条痕是"季节性斜坡纹线",即 RSL,科学家们猜测它们是由流水切割而成的,但之前一直无法进行测量。

分析 recurring slope lineae 表面意思是"反复出现的斜坡纹线"。根据上下文可知,该斜坡纹线的出现与季节相关,即在某个季节会出现,所以意译为"季节性斜坡纹线"。

对一些语义不完整的组织机构和活动名称,还应增加范畴词,使语义信息更加清晰完整。

[例·真题] Instead, she has redoubled her commitment to Emerson Collective, the organization she formed about a decade ago to make grants and investments in education initiatives and, more recently, other areas.

译文 恰恰相反,她加大了对"爱默生集体"这个慈善组织的投入。这个组织是她在大约10年前成立的,旨在为教育项目提供补助和投资,最近,该组织也开始涉足其他领域。

分析 Emerson Collective 直译为"爱默生集体",但直译后的语义是缺失的,所以根据下文中的同位定语从句,补充范畴词"这个慈善组织"。最终译为"'爱默生集体'这个慈善组织"。

15.3 报纸书名

一般而言,报纸书名常常采用直译的方法翻译。如果直译无法完全传达语义,则需要增添范畴词来进一步解释说明。

[例·真题] *The Knot* released its annual wedding survey this week, with findings showing that couples are spending a mind-numbing average of $32,641 on matrimonial celebrations.

译文 婚庆杂志《喜结连理》于本周发布了年度婚庆调查,其结果显示,情侣在婚庆典礼上平均花费 32 641 美元,这令人感到震惊。

分析 knot 有"结婚"的意思,结合上下文直译为四字格《喜结连理》。又因为 *The Knot* 是一本杂志的名字,所以增加范畴词,译为"婚庆杂志《喜结连理》"。

15.4 影视剧歌曲

影视剧歌曲的翻译一般以直译和音译为主,但同时也要兼顾艺术美和影视剧歌曲的内容。比如,将 *Anna Karenina* 音译为《安娜·卡列尼娜》,简洁明了,最大程度保留了原剧名的形式和内容,使人一看便知其主题。再比如,将 *Gone with the Wind* 意译为《乱世佳人》而不是《飘》兼顾了这部影视剧的主要内容。

[例·真题] Tucked away in this small village in Buckinghamshire County is the former Elizabethan coaching inn where William Shakespeare is said to have penned part of *A Midsummer Night's Dream*.

译文 这家前伊丽莎白时期的驿站旅馆坐落于白金汉郡的这个小村落之中,据说莎士比亚在这里书写了《仲夏夜之梦》的一部分内容。

分析 A Midsummer Night's Dream 采取了直译的方法,译为《仲夏夜之梦》。

中译英篇

中译英的主要技巧有中文句子的拆解、定语的处理、连动的处理、多层并列的处理、句子连接的处理、转译的处理，其他技巧有增减的处理、无主句的处理、主动语态的处理、重复的处理、四字结构的处理、隐喻的处理、特殊句式的处理。

16　中文句子的拆解

中英文转换中的困难很大程度上是由中英文差异造成的。中文句子形态呈竹节状,句间及句子内部的逻辑关系是隐形的;英文句子形态呈树状,句间及句子内部逻辑关系通过逻辑关系词和语法结构表现出来。因此,汉译英的一大难点就是厘清中文句子的逻辑,将其转换为中文的英文句式。一般而言,中文句子可拆解为并列结构和主从结构。

16.1　并列结构

并列结构指的是利用连词将在意义和语法上对应的多个成分或句子连接起来的结构。这种结构在英文中尤为常见,在汉译英时,可根据情况将汉语句子处理为英文并列结构。

16.1.1　句子成分并列

在英文中,句子成分并列通常包括主语并列、谓语并列、宾语并列和表语并列以及修饰语并列等情况。

[例·真题] But Ojha and colleagues created a computer program that could scrutinize individual pixels.

译文　但是,欧嘉和同事们创造了一个可以仔细查看单个像素的计算机程序。

分析　Ojha 和 colleagues 是由 and 连接的并列成分,均作本句话的主语。

在汉译英时,应准确找到句子内部的并列成分。并且,在转换为中文的英文句式时,应确保并列成分在句中的意义、位置和语法形态上是对应的。

[例·真题] 面对国际和地区形势的最新发展变化,各成员国应维护稳定、发展经济。

译文　Faced with the latest development and changes on the international and regional landscapes, all member states should safeguard their stability and boost their economy.

分析　本句话中包含三个并列成分。"国际"和"地区"是由"和"连接的并列成分,在句中作"形势"的定语。"发展"和"变化"也是并列成分,作"面对"的宾语。因为中文是意合语言,所以其间并无并列连词,翻译时需增加并列连词 and。"应维护稳定"和"(应)发展经济"是谓语并列,有共同的主语"各成员国"。因为英文不喜重复,所以第二个"应"省略。在中文的英文句式中,这三组并列成分在位置、意义上保留一一对应的关系。

[例·真题] 中国和欧洲分处欧亚大陆的两端，这块大陆是世界上面积最大的大陆，也是人口最多的大陆，市场空间广阔，发展机遇巨大。

译文 China and Europe are at the opposite ends of Eurasia, a continent that boasts the vastest landmass and the largest population in the world, which offers an immense market and promises huge development potential.

分析 本句话中出现了三个并列成分。"中国"和"欧洲"并列作句子主语；"世界上面积最大的大陆"和"人口最多的大陆"并列作"是"的主语补语，考虑到谓语动词与这两个并列结构均需构成搭配，所以将"是"译为 boast，两个主语补语处理为 boast 的并列宾语，用 and 连接。"市场空间广阔"和"发展机遇大"是修饰"大陆"的，处理为定语从句，嵌套在前一个同位定语从句中。这两个成分也是并列的，在定语从句中作并列的动宾短语，由 and 连接。

[例·真题] 中国对外援助政策坚持平等互利、共同发展、坚持与时俱进。

译文 China's foreign aid policy adheres to equality, mutual benefit, common development as well as keeping pace with the times.

分析 本句话中存在三个并列成分，均作"坚持"的宾语。根据英文行文习惯，前面的宾语通过逗号连接，最后一个宾语通过"as well as"连接。

16.1.2 句子并列——并列复合句

除了句子内部各成分间的并列外，英文句子与句子之间也可以呈并列关系，即句子并列。句子并列又称并列复合句，由两个及以上并列的分句组成。为准确理解英文并列复合句，首先要找到标点符号和并列连词，确定分句间逻辑关系，之后要找到各分句的主干和修饰成分，最后整合理解。

[例·真题] In 1978 the New Zealand Film Commission started assisting local film-makers and many films attained a world audience, some receiving international acknowledgement.

译文 1978 年，新西兰电影委员会开始支持本土电影制作人，许多电影走向世界，其中有些电影获得了国际认可。

分析 本句话可以帮助我们理解并列复合句，比较典型。此句由两个通过 and 连接的并列分句组成。第一个分句的主干是 the New Zealand Film Commission started assisting local film-makers，第二个分句的主干是 many films attained a world audience，非谓语结构 some receiving international acknowledgement 作结果状语。为体现中文意合语言的特点，翻译时可不翻译 and，将这两个并列分句处理为流水小句。

汉译英时，可将意义相关的两个或多个流水小句合并为一个并列复合句。这样既体现了英文作为形合语言的特点，又使句间逻辑关系更清晰，句意更紧凑。

[例·真题] 一切国家机关、武装力量、各政党、各社会团体、各企事业单位都必须遵守宪法和法律，任何组织或者个人都不得有超越宪法和法律的特权。

译文 All state organs, armed forces, political parties, mass organizations, enterprises, and public institutions must abide by the Constitution and the law, while no organization or individual has any privileges that transcend them.

分析 本句话由两个小句组成，分别从正、反两面叙述同一件事，因此可合并为一个由 while 引导的并列复合句。

[例·真题] 改革开放以来，中国金融业伴随现代化建设而快速成长，但实现持续发展依然任重道远。

译文 Ever since reform and opening-up, China's financial sector has enjoyed a rapid growth along with the modernization of the country, but to achieve sustainable development remains a long and arduous task.

分析 本句话由三个小句组成。"改革开放以来"是时间状语，后两个小句是并列的，可处理为由 but 连接的并列复合句。

[例·真题] 国际金融危机影响尚未消退，气候变化、粮食危机、能源资源安全、流行性疾病等全球性问题给发展中国家带来新的挑战，新形势下，中国对外援助事业任重道远。

译文 Besides the new challenges brought along by global issues such as climate change, food crisis, resource security, and epidemic disease, the impact of international financial crisis still remains, and thus China has a long way to go in providing foreign aid under this new circumstance.

分析 本句话由三个小句组成。根据句意可将该句话切分为两个并列的句子。前两个小句说的都是危机与挑战，所以合为一句话。其中第一个小句作句子主干；第二个小句处理为介词结构，作连接性状语；第三个小句与第一个小句并列，并通过 and 连接，并添加 thus 体现其间因果逻辑关系。

16.2 主从结构

主从复合句含有两个或两个以上的主谓结构，其中一套主谓结构构成句子的主干，其他主谓结构则充当句子的某个成分，如作主语、宾语、表语的名词性从句，作定语的形容词性从句或作状语的副词性从句。

16.2.1 名词性从句

顾名思义，名词性从句就是在句中充当名词成分的从句。名词性从句有四种：主语从句、宾语从句、表语从句和同位语从句。

主语从句充当主语，可放句首，由连词（that、whether）、连接代词和连接副词引导；也可放句尾，用 it 作形式主语。

宾语从句充当宾语，可直接放在谓语动词后，由连词（that、whether/if）、连接代词和连接副词引导，也可用 it 作形式宾语，将宾语从句后置。

表语从句充当表语，由连词（that、whether、as if 等）、连接代词和连接副词引导。

同位语从句充当同位语，由连词（that、whether）、连接代词和连接副词引导。

[例·真题] What many undergraduates do not know—and what so many of their professors have been unable to tell them—is how valuable the most fundamental gift of the humanities will turn out to be.

译文 许多本科生不知道——许多教授也未能告诉他们——的是，人文学科最根本的馈赠将何其宝贵。

分析 本句话可以帮助我们理解主从复合句，比较典型。主语是由 what 引导的主语从句。两个破折号之间的部分是同位语从句，解释说明前面的主语从句。主语补语是由 how 引导的表语从句。三者均属于名词性从句。

大家可以先看中文，再看英文，理解中译英的过程。中译英时，首先需找到小句中最为核心的动词作谓语动词，再将谓语动词前的主谓结构或动宾结构转换为主语从句，将谓语动词后的主谓结构或动宾结构转换为宾语从句或表语从句，将解释句中某一名词或代词的主谓或动宾结构转换为同位语从句，也可将有因果等逻辑关系的小句处理为名词性从句，并根据其逻辑关系选择合适的谓语动词连接这两个名词性从句，从而达到逻辑清晰、言简意赅的效果。

[例·真题] 有学者说贺兰口是史前人类凭借自然魅力打造的祭祀圣地，又有专家认为，贺兰口岩画是象形文字前的图画文字。

译文 Some scholars say that Helankou is a pre-historic, naturally-crafted shrine, while some others hold that Helankou rock paintings are pictograph preceding hieroglyph.

分析 本句由两个呈转折关系的小句组成，可通过表示对比的连词 while 连接。第一个小句的谓语动词确定为"说"，之后的主系补结构相应转换为"说"的宾语从句。第二个小句的谓语动词确定为"认为"，之后的主系补结构相应转换为"认为"的宾语从句。

[例·真题] 我们希望，以杭州峰会为桥梁，各国间的联系将更加紧密，世界经济的前景将更加广阔。

译文 It is our hope that the Hangzhou Summit will serve as a bridge through which countries will build stronger links with each other and together open up broader prospects for the world economy.

分析 本句话的重心是"希望"的内容，体现中文前轻后重的特点。而英文"前重后轻"，所以将"希望"后的内容处理为主语从句，将"希望"这个动词转译为同根名词。因为这个主语从句中又包含一个由后两个小句组成的定语从句，结构较为复杂，所以为避免头重脚轻，用 it 充当形式主语，将主语从句后置。

[例·真题] 地区差别和不平衡发展是中国一大问题，中西部地区地域辽阔、资源丰富、潜力巨大，是中国重要的战略发展空间、回旋余地和新的经济增长点。

译文 Despite the fact that one of the major problems China faces today is regional disparity and imbalanced development, what makes China's central and western region an important strategic space for development, convenient leeway as well as new points of economic growth is its vast territory, abundant resources and huge potential for development.

分析 本句话由三个小句组成，前一句与后两句之间呈转折关系。可将第一个小句转换为让步状语从句，而 despite 不能引导从句，所以增译范畴词 the fact，并将第一小句处理为 the fact 的同位语从句。第二个小句是第三个小句的逻辑主语，且本句强调的是"地域辽阔、资源丰富、潜力巨大"，所以可以转换句式，将这一部分处理为主语补语，将主语处理为 what 引导的主语从句。

16.2.2 形容词性从句

形容词性从句又称定语从句，是对中心词进行修饰的从句。英文定语从句的关系代词包括 who、whom、whose、that、which 和 as，这些关系代词在从句中作主语、宾语、定语和主语补语；关系副词包括 when、where、why，这些关系副词在从句中作状语。此外，"介词＋关系代词"也可以引导定语从句。

英文定语从句分为两类：限制性定语从句和非限制性定语从句。

限制性定语从句紧跟在中心词后，说明中心词的特质和身份等，是句子不可缺少的一部分，如若去除，则会导致语义缺失。非限制性定语从句通过逗号与中心词隔开，去除后不会造成语义缺失。严格来说，非限制性定语从句修饰的是整个句子，但在实际应用中，非限制性定语从句既可以修饰某个中心词，又可以修饰一整个句子。特别需要注意的是，that 只能引导限制性定语从句，而 which 既可以引导限制性定语从句，又可以引导非限制性定语从句。

[例·真题] Apple may well be the only tech company on the planet that would dare compare itself to Picasso.

译文 苹果可能是地球上唯一一家敢把自己与毕加索相提并论的科技公司。

分析 that 引导限制性定语从句，在从句中作主语。这个限制性定语从句修饰 tech company，去掉后语意不完整。

[例·真题] An early idea of theirs, which involved printing product information in fluorescent ink and reading it with ultraviolet light, proved unworkable.

译文 他们最初的想法是用荧光墨打印产品信息然后通过紫外光读取信息，但事实证明这种想法并不可行。

分析 which 引导非限制性定语从句，修饰 idea，在从句中作主语。如若去除这个非限制性定语从句，不影响句意的完性整。

汉译英时可将前后呈递进、因果等逻辑关系的两个小句处理成主从复合句，把一个小句当主句，另一个小句处理成修饰前面整句话或其中一部分的定语从句。

[例·真题] 1882年中国第一盏电灯在上海点亮，这使得中国逐渐告别了油灯和蜡烛照明的历史。

译文 In 1882, China's first electric light was turned on in Shanghai, which signaled the end of an era in which kerosene lamps and illuminating candles served as light sources.

分析 本句话由两个小句组成，前一句与后一句呈因果逻辑关系。"这"指的是前一句话这个整体，因此可将后一句话处理为非限制性定语从句，修饰前一句话。在这个非限制性定语从句中，"油灯和蜡烛照明"这个主谓结构作"历史"的定语，可处理为由 in which 引导的限制性定语从句，修饰 era。

[例·真题] 2000年，中国建成北斗导航试验系统，这使中国成为继美、俄之后世界上第三个拥有自主卫星导航系统的国家。

译文 In 2000, China successfully built the Beidou satellite navigation system, which makes it the third country that possesses indigenous satellite navigation capabilities, after the United States and Russia.

分析 本句话由三个小句组成。第一个小句是时间状语，第二个小句与第三个小句呈因果逻辑关系，且"这"指代第二个小句。因此，可将后两个小句合成一个句子，第二句作主句，第三句作非限制性定语从句修饰第二句。

[例·真题] 本美术馆以收藏、研究、展示中国近现代至当代艺术家作品为重点的国家艺术博物馆，是新中国成立以后的国家文化标志性建筑。

译文 The National Art Museum of China (NAMOC) which is dedicated to collection, research and exhibitions of modern and contemporary artistic works in China is a national cultural landmark after the founding of the People's Republic of China.

分析 句子的主干为"国家艺术博物馆是新中国成立以后的国家文化标志性建筑"，"以收藏、研究、展示中国近现代至当代艺术家作品为重点"是次要成分，且与主干联系密切，可处理成定语从句，修饰"国家艺术博物馆"。

16.2.3 副词性从句

副词性从句即状语从句，包含时间状语从句、地点状语从句、方式状语从句、条件状语从句、原因状语从句、结果状语从句、目的状语从句、让步状语从句和比较状语从句。状语从句通过连接词与主句连接，并体现与主句的逻辑关系。

[例·真题] What would happen, Mr. Woodland wondered one day, <u>if Morse code, with its elegant simplicity and limitless combinatorial potential, were adapted graphically</u>?

译文 一天伍德兰先生琢磨到,摩斯密码精巧简洁,且有无限种组合可能,<u>如果将这种密码改造成图表会怎么样呢</u>?

分析 if 引导条件状语从句。因为中文通常遵守条件—结果的逻辑关系,所以将条件状语从句放在由 what 引导的宾语从句的主句前翻译。插入语部分作定语,修饰 Morse code,这部分过长,单独处理。

汉译英时,应先确定主句,再厘清剩余小句与主句的逻辑关系,将其处理为相应的状语从句。

[例·真题] 国家行政机关要严格按照法定权限和程序办事,加快建设法治政府。

译文 State administrative organs must perform their duties in strict compliance with statutory authority and procedures <u>so that</u> the pace of developing law-based government can be accelerated.

分析 在这句话中,后一个小句是前一个小句的目的,因此,可将后一句话处理为由 so that 引导的目的状语从句,从而更清晰地体现前后两小句间的逻辑关联。

[例·真题] 同时,我们依法开展网络空间治理,网络空间日渐清朗。

译文 Meanwhile, a clean environment in the cyberspace is ensured <u>because</u> we have conducted governance of cyberspace in accordance with law.

分析 第一小句是时间状语,第二小句是第三小句的原因,所以将第二小句处理为由 because 引导的原因状语从句。而英文通常先说主句后说状语等次要信息,所以将作为主句的第三小句提至原因状语从句之前。

[例·真题] 在文字没有发明<u>前</u>,这里的人们艰难地把他们的理想、愿望、欢乐、悲伤,通过岩画的形式表现出来。

译文 <u>Before</u> written language was invented, local people expressed their ideals, wishes, happiness, and sadness in the form of pictographic signs.

分析 "在文字没有发明之前"是时间状语,因此处理成由 before 引导的时间状语从句。

17　定　语

通过前面的学习,我们已经知道中译英的本质便是如何将各个成分划分成定语或状语,因此,定语的处理是十分重要的。中文定语常位于被修饰词前,而英文定语的位置和类型多变,因此,在翻译时,可根据句意和语境灵活处理定语的位置,一般有前置和后置两种处理方式。

在翻译时,中文中可以处理为英文中定语成分的部分有几类,包括定语成分(偏正短语、动宾短语、介宾短语等)、插入语以及同位语等,可以译为相应的前置定语和后置定语。

17.1　前　置

如果中文句子中的定语是一个单词,或是结构简单、词数较少的短语,那么在翻译时通常可以不调整语序,仍采用前置译法进行翻译。

[例·真题] 近年来频发的自然灾害让全球深受其害。

译文 Frequent natural calamities over recent years have caused a heavy toll on the planet.

分析 在这句话中,形容词"频发的"和"自然"作定语,修饰中心名词"灾害",定语结构简单,翻译成英文也可以不调换语序,直接前置处理为 frequent natural calamities。

17.2　后　置

如果中文句子中的定语成分较为复杂,则翻译时通常采用后置译法进行处理。由于英文定语成分类型多样,故中文定语可以根据语法和句意的需要,译为不定式、of 结构、介词短语、分词短语、定语从句、同位语或插入语等多种形式。

[例·真题] 现在,以互联网为代表的信息技术日新月异,引领了社会生产新变革,创造了人类生活新空间,拓展了国家治理新领域,极大提高了人类认识世界、改造世界的能力。

译文 Today the ever-changing information technology, represented by the Internet, has transformed production and added new dimensions to human life. It also opened up a new frontier for the state governance and enhanced our ability to understand and transform the world.

分析 这句话的翻译涉及两处定语的处理。第一处是"以互联网为代表的信息技术日新月异",其中,"以互联网为代表"为定语,修饰中心名词"信息技术",可以译为分词,作后置定语,即 represented by the Internet,而"日新月异"也可以处理为形容词作前置定语修饰中心名词,即 ever-changing。第二处是"人类认识世界、改造世界的能力",可以处理成不定式的形式作后置定语,即 the ability to understand and transform the world。

[例·真题] 2000年,中国建成北斗导航试验系统,这使中国成为继美、俄之后世界上第三个拥有自主卫星导航系统的国家。

译文 Following the establishment of the Beidou Navigation Experimental System in 2000, China has joined the United States and Russia as the only countries with home-grown satnav systems.

分析 翻译这句话之前,首先要确定定语部分和状语部分。"2000年,中国建成北斗导航试验系统"作为背景信息,可以处理为原因状语。剩余部分可以进行转换,即"中国是美、俄之外的唯一一个拥有自主卫星导航系统的国家",那么需要处理的定语部分则为"拥有自主卫星导航系统",修饰的中心名词为"国家"。这里可以采用介词结构作定语,译为 with home-grown satnav systems。

[例·真题] 浙江杭州是风景秀美之地,也是创新活力之城。

译文 Hangzhou is a land of scenic beauty, as well as a city of innovation and change.

分析 在这句话中,"之"有"的"的意思,所以可以将汉语原句转换为"浙江杭州是风景秀美的地方,也是有创新活力的城市"。句中有两个定语"风景秀美"和"创新活力",在这里可以处理为 of 结构的后置定语,即 a land of scenic beauty 和 a city of innovation and change,最后得到上述译文。

[例·真题] 互联网让世界变成了"鸡犬之声相闻"的地球村,相隔万里的人们不再"老死不相往来"。

译文 The Internet has turned the world into a global village where distance is not the barriers to prevent people from interacting with each other anymore.

分析 在翻译过程中,首先确定中心名词是"地球村",其次对句意进行合并,定语部分过长,故可以采用后置译法,译为从句,由 where 引导。

除了将汉语中的定语成分处理为英文中相应的定语成分外,由于汉语中往往会存在隐含的逻辑关系,如假设、因果、转折、让步或解释说明等,所以在译成英文时也可以译为相应的定语从句。

[例·真题] 我们希望,以杭州峰会为桥梁,各国间的联系将更加紧密,世界经济的前景将更加广阔。

译文 We hope that the Hangzhou Summit will serve as a bridge through which countries will build stronger links with each other and deliver a brighter prospect for the world economy.

分析 这个例子很好地体现了汉译英的本质是处理成定语和状语。"以杭州峰会为桥梁"是原句中的方式状语,在翻译时,可以将其处理成主句,再将原句中的主语"各国间联系……广阔"处理为定语从句,由引导词 through which 来体现其中的逻辑关系,最终得到上述译文。

[例] 唯有牛顿这个在人类历史上具有伟大影响的科学家,才能够思潮奔腾,才华迸发,敢于思考前人从未思考过的问题,敢于踏进前人从未涉足的领域。

译文 Only Newton, an immensely influential scientist in human history, is empowered to bring out his best, emboldening to think creatively and enter unchartered territories.

分析 在这句话中,定语为"这个在人类历史上具有伟大影响的科学家",修饰中心名词"牛顿"。在这里可以处理为同位语的形式,即 an immensely influential scientist in human history,从而使译文更为贴合英语的表达习惯。

18　连　动

汉语连动句是指谓语动词由多个动词构成,共同陈述同一个主语的汉语句子。这些谓语动词之间的逻辑关系十分复杂。因此,处理这种汉语句子的第一步便是厘清各谓语动词之间的关系。一般而言,若这些谓语动词之间是并列关系,则采用并列连词连接,共同作英语句子中的谓语动词。如果是主从关系,则只保留一个动词作英语中的谓语动词,其他动词处理为非谓语动词、介词短语或不定式等结构。

18.1　并列连动

并列式连动句中的动词一般同时或先后发生,通常可将其全部处理为由并列连词串连起来的英语谓语动词。

[例·真题] 积极稳妥<u>推进</u>城镇化,<u>发挥</u>城镇化对扩内需、促发展、惠民生的潜力作用。

译文 We will actively <u>push forward</u> urbanization in a stable manner and <u>unleash</u> its potential to expand domestic demand, promote development and improve living standards of local residents.

分析 汉语原句中,"推进""发挥"这两个动词是同时发出的,呈并列关系,因此,译文中将二者均保留,作谓语动词,用并列连词 and 连接。

[例·真题] 我们应该<u>恪守</u>联合国宪章宗旨和原则,充分<u>发挥</u>联合国及其安理会在维护和平、缔造和平、建设和平方面的核心作用。

译文 We should <u>abide by</u> the purposes and principles of the UN Charter and <u>bring into full play</u> the central role of the United Nations and its Security Council in peace keeping, peace making, and peace building.

分析 "恪守"和"发挥"在同一语义层级且不分主次,呈并列关系,因此将二者均处理为谓语动词,并用 and 连接。

18.2　从属连动

从属连动句中的动词有主次之分。在汉译英时需先确定主要动词,将其作为谓语动词,将次要动词处理为非谓语动词、介词短语、不定式等结构。

[例·真题] 早在 1996 年,中国就启动实施了"绿色照明工程",中国绿色照明工程的实施,推动了照明电器行业结构的优化升级和产品质量的整体提升。

译文 In 1996, China launched the Green Lighting Project, thus pushing forward the structural upgrading of the lighting industry and the improvement of product quality.

分析 本句中有两个动词,即"启动实施"和"推动"。这两个动词并非并列关系,而是有主次之分。根据句意,将"启动实施"定为谓语动词,"推动"与前一句话存在因果逻辑关系,所以处理为非谓语动词结构。

[例·真题] 因此,我们要采取以下措施,切实保障宪法和法律的有效实施。

译文 Therefore, we should adopt the following measures to ensure the effective enforcement of the Constitution and laws.

分析 在本句话中,后一句话是前一句话的目的,所以将前一句话作为句子主干,将"要采取"作为谓语动词,并把"切实保障"处理为不定式结构,作目的状语。

18.3 链式联动

链式联动句指的是同一主语按照逻辑、时间先后等顺序进行一系列动作的句子,体现了汉语作为意合语言的特点。链式联动句动词间的相互关系隐含在语义中。英语是形合的语言,会通过语法、逻辑连接词等体现动词间的关系。在翻译链式联动句时,首先要确定最核心动词(作谓语动词),再根据其他动词与谓语动词的语义逻辑关系,转换动词为介词结构、非谓语动词等形态,并注意动词的时态,通过时态展现链式联动关系。

[例·真题] 去年冬天至今,俄罗斯人先是经历冬天的严寒,随后是春旱和火灾,如今旱涝齐至。

译文 From last winter to date, Russians have lived through freezing winter cold followed by spring drought and wildfires, and then by a mix of droughts and flooding which are happening now.

分析 本句中的三个动作按照先后顺序展开。保留"经历",作谓语动词;将"随后是"处理为非谓语动词"followed by",作"严寒"的后置定语,也体现了二者的先后关系;再将"齐至"处理为后置定语,修饰"旱涝",并通过现在进行时和 then 体现出动作在时间上的先后顺序。

[例·真题] 2000 多年前,亚欧大陆上勤劳勇敢的人民探索出多条连接亚欧非几大文明的贸易和人文交流通路,后人将其统称为"丝绸之路"。

译文 Over 2000 years ago, industrious and courageous people on the Eurasian continent discovered a raft of passages linking major civilizations in Asia, Europe, and Africa for trade and cultural exchanges, which are later collectively referred to as the "Silk Road".

分析 "探索出"和"称为"这两个谓语动词虽然在语义上是并列的,但在时间上却是先后发生的,因此,将"探索出"译为 discovered,将"称为"译为 are referred to,通过时态展现链式联动关系。

19　多层并列

中文是意合语言，常常会使用大量并列结构，且这些并列结构之间很少有连接词来体现其间的逻辑关系。英文是形合语言，逻辑关系常常通过连接词等体现出来。因此，汉译英的关键在于正确理解各并列结构之间的逻辑关系。首先需要确定句子主干，再以逻辑关系为依据，确定选词并合理添加连接词，也可以灵活变换句式。

19.1　厘清主干

首先要根据上下文和句意确定多层并列结构的重点，并将其转换为七种英文句式的其中一种，作句子主干。需要注意的有两点：第一，由于汉语中存在无主句，缺少主语，所以在厘清多层并列结构的主干信息时，需要根据语境补出其逻辑主语，或者有时出于保持句子客观性的需要，采用被动语态，用物作主语；第二，要注意多层并列结构中并列谓语动词的时态要保持一致。

[例·真题] 同时，深化境外战略投资者与中资银行的合作，稳步推进股票、债券、保险市场对外开放，促进人民币跨境使用，逐步实现人民币资本项目可兑换，拓展金融业对外开放的广度和深度。

译文　In the meantime, we will deepen cooperation between Chinese banks and their foreign strategic investors, open the stock, bond, and insurance markets in an orderly way, promote the cross-border use of the RMB, and achieve the RMB's convertibility under the capital account gradually and expand the breadth and depth of opening-up in the financial sector.

分析　这句话是政经文本中典型的多重并列结构，分析句子结构时可先厘清其主干部分。这句话是一个汉语无主句，可增添泛指代词"我们"作主语；主语对应的五个并列谓语动词分别是"深化""推进""促进""实现""拓展"，五个谓语动词均采用将来时态；这五个谓语动词对应的宾语分别是"合作""开放""使用""可兑换""广度和深度"。主谓宾确定后，可将剩余部分处理为修饰成分。根据句意可知，这五个谓语动词在逻辑上是并列的，所以此句多重并列结构可处理为这样的结构：we will deepen ..., open ..., promote ..., achieve ..., and expand... 。

[例·真题] 应该本着求同存异的原则，尊重各国主权和选择发展道路和发展模式的权利，尊重文明多样性，在交流互鉴、取长补短中相得益彰、共同进步。

> **译文** In line with the principle of seeking common ground while shelving differences, we should respect the sovereignty of all countries and their right to choose their own development paths and models. And we should respect the diversity of civilizations, achieve win-win development and pursue common progress through mutual learning and drawing on each other's strength.

> **分析** 本句话由四个无主语小句组成，因为本句话过长，可断成两个小句。首先增添泛指代词 we，作主语。"应该本着求同存异的原则"是方式状语，处理为介词结构。"尊重""尊重""相得益彰"和"取长"并列作谓语动词。综上，此句多重并列结构可处理为这样的结构：we should respect... and we should respect... , achieve... and pursue... 。

19.2 注意选词

多层并列结构中的并列部分力求选词准确、搭配合理、语法正确。第一，由于多层并列结构中存在多个并列的谓语动词和宾语，汉译英时要注意一一对应搭配，不能错位；第二，由于中文中有些动宾搭配不符合英文表达习惯，所以此时要根据句意调整，保持搭配合理性；最后，在翻译选词时应注意词性的一致性，加强语言表达的修辞美和语法的严密性。

> **[例·真题]** 现在，以互联网为代表的信息技术日新月异，引领了社会生产新变革，创造了人类生活新空间，拓展了国家治理新领域，极大提高了人类认识世界、改造世界的能力。

> **译文** Today, information technologies represented by the Internet are experiencing rapid changes with each passing day. They have brought about new ways of social production, created new space for people's life, opened new horizons of state governance, and enhanced our ability to understand and shape the world.

> **分析** "日新月异"是抽象的中文四字格，形容发展、变化速度快，每天都有变化。译为 experience rapid changes with each passing day，既体现了原意，也保留了夸张的修辞。"引领新变革"按照字面翻译是 lead new revolution，这是无法准确表达出原文"带来了新的社会生产发展方式"的深层含义的，且"引领变革"这种搭配是不合适的，所以将其意译为 brought about new ways。再者还需注意动宾搭配。此句有两处并列的动宾结构，"创造"和"空间"搭配，"提高"和"能力"搭配，动宾搭配要一一对应，这样才能合理搭配。此外，也要注意"新变革""新空间""新领域""能力"这四个宾语的选词一致性，加强语言表达的修辞美和语法严密性。因此，将其分别译为 brought about new ways、created new space、opened new horizons、enhanced our ability。

19.3 合理连接

由于中文中的多层并列结构常通过逗号而不是逻辑连词连接，所以在将中文转换为英文句式时需要选择合适的逻辑连词来合理串联起各并列结构,避免一味地使用 and。

[例·真题] 国家审判机关、检察机关要依法独立公正行使审判权、检察权,维护社会公平正义。

译文 State judicial and procuratorial organs must exercise their judicial and procuratorial powers in an independent and just manner so that social equity and justice are firmly upheld.

分析 "国家审判机关"和"检察机关""独立"和"公正""审判权"和"检察权"之间都是并列关系,所以用"and"连接。该句由两个小句组成,看似是并列的,实则后一句话是前一句话的目的,所以用 so that 合理连接前后两个小句,而不是 and,如果仅使用 and,则整句中的 and 会太多,并列结构的分层也就变得复杂含混起来。

[例·真题] 兼有部分古代书画和外国艺术作品,同时也包括丰富的民间美术作品。

译文 Collections also include some ancient paintings and calligraphy works, foreign artistic works as well as plentiful folk art works.

分析 本句由两个并列小句组成,并列小句中又包含着并列的短语结构。如果并列的小句和短语结构全部使用 and 来连接,那么译文将会显得非常笨拙和枯燥,因此本句中用 and 来连接第一层的并列结构,用 as well as 来连接第二层的并列结构,使整句结构更为清晰,层次也更加分明。

19.4 灵活变换

多层并列结构句式除了处理为并列句,还可以根据上下文语义和逻辑灵活变换为介词结构、非谓语结构等,在句中充当修饰成分。

[例·真题] 自 21 年前接入国际互联网以来,我们按照积极利用、科学发展、依法管理、确保安全的思路,加强信息基础设施建设,发展网络经济,推进信息惠民。

译文 Since China was connected to World Wide Web 21 years ago, we, in accordance with the principles of proactive utilization, rational development, law-based regulation, and assurance of security, have strengthened IT infrastructure, developed cyber economy and made life better for our people through IT application.

分析 本句由三层并列结构组成。由句意和隐含的逻辑关系可知,"按照积极利用、科学发展、依法管理、确保安全的思路"是"加强信息基础设施建设,发展网络经济,推进信息惠民"的方式状语;"自 21 年前接入国际互联网以来"是时间状语。因此,将第三个小句确定为句子主干,将第一个小句处理为由 since 引导的时间状语从句,将第二个小句处理为介词结构(作方式状语)。

[例·真题] 来自全国和世界各地的商品源源不断地进入西藏,丰富着城乡市场和百姓生活。

译文 Commodities from all over the nation and across the world keep flowing into Tibet, enriching the urban and rural markets as well as the lives of the people.

分析 前后两小句呈因果逻辑关系,因此可以将第一小句作主干,将第二小句处理为非谓语结构(作结果状语)。

20　句子的连接

通过前面的学习,我们知道了英汉两种语言之间的差异:汉语是意合的语言,呈竹节状,短句较多;而英语是形合的语言,呈树状,多用长句。因此,在汉译英时,通常先厘清汉语句子中各个小句之间的信息,分析和确定句子当中的逻辑关系,再根据具体语意选用词或短语、非谓语动词、从句等结构来实现句子的连接,使其成为彼此之间拥有明确逻辑关系的长句。

20.1　词或短语

[例·真题] 2010年,中国稀土开采总量控制指标为89 200吨,同比增长8.4%;稀土产品出口配额为3.03万吨,同比下降39.5%。

译文 The rare earth exploitation of China is capped at 89,200 tons in 2010, up 8.4% year-on-year, while the rare earth export quota stands at 30,300 tons, down 39.5% year-on-year.

分析 在这句话中,以分号分隔的两个分句构成转折的逻辑关系。因为英文中多用长句,所以可以考虑使用表转折含义的连词(如while)连接两个大分句,表示对比,从而得到上述译文。

[例·真题] 中国是世界上最大的发展中国家,人口多,底子薄,经济发展不平衡。

译文 China is the world's largest developing country, with a large population, a poor foundation and uneven economic development.

分析 在这句话中,"人口多,底子薄,经济发展不平衡"都是对"中国是世界上最大的发展中国家"的解释说明,翻译成英文后可作解释性状语,通过短语的方式将中文短句连接起来。

20.2　非谓语动词

常见的用于连接句子的非谓语动词有分词、过去分词、不定式等。分词和过去分词的选用主要取决于动词和主语之间的主被动关系,主动关系则用分词,被动关系则用过去分词。

[例·真题] 中国对外援助坚持平等互利,注重实效,与时俱进,不附带任何政治条件,形成了具有自身特色的模式。

译文 Adhering to equality and mutual benefit, stressing substantial results, and keeping pace with the times without imposing any political conditions on recipient countries, China's foreign aid has emerged as a model with its own characteristics.

分析 "中国对外援助形成了具有自身特色的模式"为主干,"坚持平等互利,注重实效,与时俱进,不附带任何政治条件"为方式状语。由于"坚持"和主语"中国"呈主动关系,翻译成英文时可以考虑将其译为现在分词短语的形式,将原句中的短句连接起来。

[例·真题] 虽然北斗卫星导航系统是中国独立发展、自主运行的卫星导航系统,但这并不影响它与世界上其他卫星导航系统之间的兼容性。

译文 Independently developed and operated by China, yet Beidou is compatible with other satellite navigation systems in the world.

分析 首先进行句意整理,"北斗卫星导航系统"是由"中国"发展和运行的,二者之间构成被动的关系,故选用过去分词短语连接两个分句。

[例·真题] 因此,我们要采取以下措施,切实保障宪法和法律的有效实施。

译文 Therefore, we need to take the following measures to genuinely guarantee the effective enforcement of the Constitution and laws.

分析 在这句话中,"切实保障宪法和法律的有效实施"是目的状语,翻译成英文时可以考虑将其译为不定式的形式与主句相连接。

20.3 从 句

[例·真题] 2000年,中国建成北斗导航试验系统,这使中国成为继美、俄之后世界上第三个拥有自主卫星导航系统的国家。

译文 In 2000, China completed the BeiDou Navigation Satellite System (BDS), thus making it the third country that possessed indigenous satellite navigation system in the world after the United States and Russia.

分析 在这句话中,由于在分句"这使中国成为继美、俄之后世界上第三个拥有自主卫星导航系统的国家"中,"国家"的定语部分过长,在翻译时可以进行后置处理,译为定语从句,从而将句子连接起来。

[例·真题] 我们希望,以杭州峰会为桥梁,各国间的联系将更加紧密,世界经济的前景将更加广阔。

译文 We hope that the Hangzhou Summit can serve as a bridge that brings countries closer together and makes global economic prospects ever brighter.

分析 在这句话中,"以杭州峰会为桥梁,各国间的联系将更加紧密,世界经济的前景将更加广阔"为宾语,在翻译时可以译为宾语从句;在后面的各个分句当中,"各国间的联系……更加广阔"可以作为定语,修饰中心词"桥梁"。定语从句使各个分句连接起来,也使句子间的逻辑更为紧密。

21 转 译

如前文所言,转译在本质上是一个润色的过程。在汉译英时,如果保留原文词类使行文不通,则可采取转译的策略,改变词类。前文提到过,英译汉的转译一般发生在名词、动词、形容词和副词之间,汉译英亦是如此。一般而言,汉译英的转译包含以下情况:汉语动词转为英语名词,汉语动词转为英语形容词、副词,汉语形容词转为英语名词,汉语名词转为英语动词,以及范畴词转译。

21.1 动转名

在第1章中,我们提到过,汉英的差异之一在于动静。汉语是动态的语言,善用动词;而英语是静态的语言,喜用名词、介词短语等。因此,在汉译英时,常常把汉语动词转译为英语名词。

[例·真题] 改革开放以来,中国金融业伴随现代化建设而快速成长,但实现持续发展依然任重道远。

译文 Since the beginning of reform and opening-up, China's financial sector has enjoyed rapid growth along with the modernization of the country, but to achieve sustainable development remains a long and arduous task.

分析 "成长"是动词,可转译为同根名词 growth,并增添 enjoy 这个弱动词作谓语动词。"伴随现代化建设"是方式状语,可处理为介词短语,将"伴随"这个动词转译为介词 along with,将"现代化建设"转译为名词 modernization。"实现持续发展"是"但"连接的并列复合句中第二个小句的主语,是动词性质的,而英文中,动宾结构不能作主语,所以将其转译为不定式结构 to achieve sustainable development。"任重道远"是动词性质的四字格,转译为有形容词修饰的名词 a long and arduous task,并增添 remain 这个弱动词作谓语动词。

[例·真题] 第二次世界大战结束以来,世界经济能够快速增长,主要得益于相对和平稳定的国际环境。

译文 Since the end of the Second World War, the rapid growth of the world economy is the result of a relatively peaceful and stable international environment.

分析 本句中有三个动词,即"结束""增长"和"得益于",均可转译为名词,转译后的名词分别为 end、growth 和 result。这充分体现了英文作为静态语言的特点。

21.2 动转形副

在汉语中，某些表示状态的动词可以转换为形容词或副词并与其他动词搭配，这样既符合英文静态语言的习惯，又避免了啰嗦繁复。

[例·真题] 2010年，中国稀土开采总量控制指标为89 200吨，同比增长8.4%；稀土产品出口配额为3.03万吨，同比下降39.5%。

译文 The rare earth exploitation of China is capped at 89,200 tons in 2010, up 8.4% year-on-year, while the export quota stands at 30,300 tons, down 39.5% year-on-year.

分析 "增长"和"下降"均为动词，如要保持其动词词性，只能另起一句。这会削弱该部分与主句的逻辑关系，并且导致句式繁杂。而且，这两个动词在此句中均起修饰作用。所以，可将这两个动词分别译为副词up和down。

[例·真题] 面对复杂的国际和地区形势，维护地区安全稳定和促进成员国共同发展，过去、现在乃至将来相当长时期内都是上海合作组织的首要任务和目标。

译文 In the face of complex regional and international situation, it was, is and will be SCO's top priority task and target to protect regional security and stability, as well as promote common development to all the members for a considerable period.

分析 句子的主干：维护地区安全稳定和促进成员国共同发展，过去、现在乃至将来相当长时期内都是上海合作组织的首要任务和目标。第一个小句可处理为解释状语，其中的动词"面对"可以转译为副词性质的介词结构 in the face of，避免了过于生硬的表述，从而符合英语表达习惯。

21.3 形转名

在汉译英时，可根据上下文语境及表达需要，将汉语中的形容词转换为英语中的同根名词。

[例·真题] 事实上，人类正处于极端天气的适应期。

译文 In fact, human beings are adapting to extreme weather patterns.

分析 "极端天气的"是形容词，修饰"适应期"。"正处于极端天气的适应期"，即正在适应极端天气。所以，此处将"极端天气的"这个形容词转译为名词extreme weather patterns，为配合转译后的名词，将"适应期"转译为同根动词adapt，作谓语动词。

[例·真题] 中国将与世界各国一道为建设持久和平、共同繁荣的和谐世界而不懈努力。

译文 China, together with other countries in the world, will spare no efforts in building a harmonious world of enduring peace and common prosperity.

分析 "持久和平"和"共同繁荣"均作"和谐世界"的定语。因为这两个四字格较为复杂,所以将其转译为名词词组 enduring peace and common prosperity,并用 of 引导,放在中心词后,作后置定语。

21.4 名转动

在汉译英时,常常是动词转名词,但是名词转动词的现象也是存在的。应根据英文表达习惯和上下文来决定是否进行转译和如何进行转译,而不是墨守成规。名词转动词的现象在 CATTI 二级笔译考试中也多次出现。

[例·真题] 中欧在不同文明包容互鉴中可以成为引领。

译文 China and the EU could lead the way in accommodation and mutual learning from different civilizations.

分析 "引领"是名词,为句子的宾语成分,可以在翻译时将"引领"转译为英语动词词组 lead the way,使句子的表述精准又自然。

[例·真题] 2000 年,中国建成北斗导航试验系统,这使中国成为继美、俄之后世界上第三个拥有自主卫星导航系统的国家。

译文 China's successful construction of the BeiDou Navigation Satellite System in 2000 makes it the third country possessed of indigenous satellite navigation capabilities, after the US and Russia.

分析 句子的主干为"这使中国成为国家"。"这"代指前面一整句话,可将其处理为名词性质的短语作句子主语,所以可将"建成"转译为名词 construction,将"中国"和"北斗导航试验系统"处理为定语,修饰 construction。此外,"第三个拥有自主卫星导航系统的"是"国家"的定语,可将动词"拥有"转译为形容词 possessed,并和"北斗导航试验系统"一并作"国家"的后置定语。

21.5 范畴词转译

汉语常用表示现象、属性、状况等的范畴词,以使句意完整。范畴词本身无实意,常跟在形容词、名词和动词后面。而在英语中,后缀为 -tion、-ty、-ment、-ness 等的抽象名词本身就有范畴词的含义和作用。因此,汉译英时常常省略中文中的范畴词。

[例·真题] 因此,我们要在继续加强立法工作的同时,采取积极有效的措施,切实保障宪法和法律的有效实施。

译文 Therefore, we need to take active and effective measures to ensure the implementation of the Constitution and other laws at the same time of strengthening legislation.

分析 "加强立法工作"的"工作"是范畴词，翻译时采取省译法。

针对中文中范畴词的英译，除了省译法，有时还会采取转译法，将带有范畴词的句子换一种说法。

[例·真题] 我们要大力推动流动人口基本公共服务均等化，着力提升流动人口服务管理水平，确保流动人口公平公正地享受城镇公共资源和社会福利。

译文 We strengthen our efforts to provide equal access to basic public services and better management of services for the migrant population to ensure that they have a fair and equal access to urban public resources and social welfare.

分析 "流动人口服务管理水平"中的"水平"是明显的范畴词，直译成 level 会造成行文不通。因此，我们可以调整句子结构，将其转译为"为流动人口提供更好的服务管理"。

22 增　减

由于英汉两种语言间的差异，我们在翻译过程中绝不能只是简单地词对词直译，而是需要根据不同语言的表达习惯进行调整，包括适当地增词或减词，从而让译文更加符合其语言特点。在汉译英过程中，常见增词、减词的情况有：语法增减、语意增减、语体增减、范畴词省译等。

22.1　语法增减

汉英语法差异主要体现在冠词、介词、助词、关联词等方面。汉语中没有冠词，而英语中有；汉语少用介词，而英语中的介词搭配十分常见；汉语少用关联词，多是隐含的逻辑关系，而英语作为形合语言则常用关联词……因此，汉译英时应当根据具体的语境来判断，进行适当的语法增减。

[例·真题] 中国节能灯产品质量水平日益提高，一些企业产品质量和工艺水平已达到世界领先水平。

译文　The quality of Chinese energy-efficient lights have improved dramatically, and the technological level and quality standards of some manufacturers now lead the world.

分析　在这句话中，前后句之间是并列关系，而中文中并没有出现明显的关联词。考虑到汉英语言的表达差异，在翻译时，需要添加关联词 and 来体现句子之间的逻辑关系。

22.2　语意增减

语意指语言所蕴含的意义。翻译过程中的语意增减是指不能字对字直译，而要根据实际情况判断，是否需要增词或减词。

[例·真题] 作为看漫画长大的 80 后一代，热爱传统居民建筑的毛葛想到了通过漫画形式向人们介绍传统民居，希望让更多人看到传统居民建筑的美并加入到保护传统民居的行列。

译文　As someone born in the 1980s and a big fan of traditional houses, Mao grew up reading comic books like her peers. Therefore, this girl came up an idea that traditional houses can be presented in the form of comics so as to expose their beauty to more people and encourage them to join the protection campaign.

分析 在这句话中，"看"出现了两次，这里的"看"并不是简单的字面意思"look"，更多的是表达其引申义：第一个"看漫画"，则是指"读漫画"，也就是"reading"；第二个"看到……的美"，则是指把这份美呈现在人们面前，也就是"expose sth. to sb."。增加或是替换的词汇把"看"这个动词诠释得更为透彻，还满足了句式结构的美观性和语法性需求。

[例·真题] 凭着自己对社会现实的理解与感悟，对美好生活的追求与向往，把自己的亲身感受与体验，忠实地记录在岩石之上，同时也为后人留下了神秘瑰丽的贺兰山岩画。

译文 Based on their understanding of the world and driven by their pursuit of a better life, the early settlers kept an authentic record of their experiences on rocks and in doing so, left beautiful and mysterious rock art in the Helan mountains for those to come.

分析 在这句话中，"理解"与"感悟""追求"与"向往""感受"与"体验"三组词的语义相近。在翻译时，为使语言更加简洁精炼，需要进行语义减词，翻译其中一个即可。

22.3 语体增减

语体，即语言的特点，包括句式结构、修辞手段等。汉语为了满足读者思维和审美预期，往往有艺术渲染和复杂冗余的语言特点。在翻译过程中，对这些成分通常采取省略或意译的手法，从而使译文信息明确、结构合理；反之，对汉语句子中的重要信息，为起到强调等修辞目的，翻译时需要适当地进行增译，从而凸显其重要性。

[例·真题] 炎热的酷暑、狂暴的飓风、刺骨的严寒以及滔天的洪水近乎成了"常客"，风调雨顺已被视为"奢侈品"。

译文 Extreme heat, violent hurricanes, severe cold and devastating floods have become normal, and favorable weather conditions are rare to see.

分析 在这句话中，"常客"是用来修饰人的，"奢侈品"是用来修饰物的，这里都把它们用来修饰天气这一自然条件，凸显了环境的恶劣，满足了中文极具审美性的语言特点。翻译时，可以采取意译的翻译方法。

[例·真题] 2008年四川汶川大地震后，灾区电话无法接通，手机信号中断。

译文 In the wake of the devastating earthquake in Wenchuan, Sichuan Province in 2008, telecommunication services in stricken areas were cut off as a result of interrupted mobile signals.

分析 "四川汶川大地震"是一个非常惨痛的经历，为强调其破坏力之大，在翻译时可以进行增译，用 devastating 来增添文章的语体色彩。

22.4 范畴词省译

在英译汉的过程中通常会添加范畴词,那么相应的,在汉译英的过程中,也需要对范畴词进行省译。

[例·真题] 中国特色社会主义法律体系的形成,总体上解决了有法可依的问题,在这种情况下,有法必依、执法必严、违法必究的问题就显得更为突出,更加紧迫。

译文 As the established socialist legal system with Chinese characteristics ensures that there are laws to go by, it is more important to ensure that laws are observed and strictly enforced, with law breakers reliably prosecuted.

分析 在这句话中,"问题"就是一个很典型的范畴词,若将其译为 the problem of,那么译文就会十分复杂繁琐,但"问题"本身并不影响句意的表达,所以在翻译时可以采取省译的方法,省略范畴词,并将其前面的名词或形容词译为抽象名词或词组,从而使译文更加简洁明了。

23　无主句

汉语重视意合,不强调句子形态的完整性,因此在政府公文、科技文本等文体中常出现无主句。英语重视形合,即句子形式和结构要完整。在处理汉语无主句时,需将缺失的句子结构补充完整,使翻译出来的英文句子符合形态完整的要求。汉语无主句的翻译一般可以采用四种方法:补主语、译被动、找主语和换句型。

23.1　补主语

汉语无主句从形式上省略了句子的主语,但在内容上却暗含着隐性的逻辑主语,翻译为英语时需根据句子前后逻辑或结合上下文语境将隐性逻辑主语补齐,译为主动语态。

[例·真题] 坚持通过对话和协商,以和平方式解决国际争端。

译文 We should settle international disputes in peace through dialogue and consultation.

分析 根据前文"我们应该"可以推断出这里的隐性逻辑主语也是"我们",所以翻译时增加逻辑主语 we。

23.2　译被动

在政治或法律这类严肃文本中,汉语无主句并不强调行为施动者,而仅仅强调行为本身,因此翻译为英语时也无需刻意找到隐性主语,只需用被动语态将行为本身叙述出来即可,这样译文既能忠实于原句内容,又能符合形式上的客观性。

[例·真题] 二要坚持依法行政和公正司法。

译文 Second, law-based administration and judicial justice should be adhered to.

分析 本句话强调的是"坚持依法行政和公正司法"这个动作,并不强调施动者,所以将其转换为被动语态。

23.3　找主语

有时,汉语无主句中的其他成分(比如宾语、状语等)也可以作句子主语,发出谓语动词所代表的动作;还有时,无主句的谓语动词本身有同根名词,可直接将汉语的动词转译为名词,并根据上下文补充新的动词作谓语动词。

[例] 推动建立上海合作组织开发银行,为本组织基础设施建设和经贸合作项目提供融资保障和结算平台。

译文 The push for the establishment of SCO Development Bank will provide a financing vehicle and settlement platform for infrastructure construction and business cooperation among SCO members.

分析 本句话是由两个无主句组成的并列复合句。但根据句间逻辑关系可知,前后两句话中包含因果逻辑关系,可合并为一个句子,将前一个无主句处理为后一个无主句的主语,把"推动"和"建立"转译为同根名词 push 和 establishment。

23.4 换句型

若以上三种方法应用效果不佳,则可根据句意以及上下文语境将汉语无主句改变为英语中的特殊句型,比如倒装、强调、祈使句、各种从句等,使译文更加灵活,自然。

[例] 据考证,贺兰口岩画是不同时期先后刻制的。

译文 It is suggested by archeological findings that Helankou paintings were carved at different periods of time.

分析 这句话强调"考证"的内容,而不是施动者,所以将"考证"的内容处理为主语从句,并用 it 作形式主语,避免头重脚轻。

24　主动变被动

当句子主语所指的人或物是动作的承受者时,谓语动词的形式就是被动语态。英语中常见被动语态,而汉语中主动语态偏多,也常用主动语态来表达被动含义。因而在汉译英过程中,要根据原句的功能及其表达的含义,适当地进行主动变被动的处理,常见的有以下几种情况。

24.1　实质被动句

在汉语中,有些句子虽然没有出现"被"字,但其内容本质上包含着被动的意义;还有些句子在翻译时出于句意通顺和语言习惯的需要,会变换句子中的主语,因此产生被动现象。

[例·真题] 1882年中国第一盏电灯在上海点亮。

译文 In 1882, China's first electric lamp was turned on in Shanghai.

分析 在这句话中,主语为"电灯",谓语动词为"点亮",二者之间很显然为被动关系,即"电灯被点亮"。故在翻译时需要译出其被动关系。

[例·真题] 中医药在历史发展进程中,形成了独特的生命观。

译文 The unique views on life were created through the long history of TCM's development.

分析 在这句话中,根据语言表达习惯,翻译时变换主语为"生命观",与原句中的谓语动词"形成"构成了被动关系。

24.2　"是"字句

在汉语中,有些句子的结构为"是+动词+的",并且逻辑上的施动主语不详,而且句子内容较客观,大多为事实,在汉译英时可将其译为被动语态。

[例·真题] 在世界上,中国岩画是诞生最早的。

译文 Among the world, Chinese rock painting has been created as the earliest one.

24.3 主语泛指句

汉语中的一些句子会存在泛指主语（如"人们""大家""大众"等），而句子的重点内容则为泛指主语后的客观事实。在这种情况下，汉译英时可将汉语的主动语态翻译为英语的被动语态，同时省略施动主语（如somebody、everyone等），以凸显泛指主语后的句子重点。

[例] 人们大都认为一个好的老师可以改变一个人一生的命运。

译文 A good teacher is commonly believed to be able to change one's fate.

分析 这句话中存在泛指主语"人们"，翻译时可省略，同时将主动语态变为被动语态。

24.4 正式委婉句

在汉语中，有些句子内容为命令、通知、公告类，语气较正式；有些句子内容则为邀请、请求类，语气较委婉。此类型句子往往无主语或是主语在句中不作重要成分，所以在汉译英时通常可以将此类句子译为英语的被动语态形式，从而更加贴合语言习惯、凸显语意。

[例] 进入公共场所请出示健康码。

译文 Health code is requested for entering public places.

24.5 特殊无主句

在汉语中，有些句子的开头由"据说/据报道/据考证……"等构成，在这种情况下的汉译英一般采用"it is＋过去分词＋that从句"的被动语态形式，从而更好地体现句子的重点和语义。

[例·真题] 据考证，贺兰山口岩画是不同时期先后刻制的。

译文 It was proved that Helan Mountain Pass rock engravings were produced successively at different times.

25 重复

汉语重意合，强调语言的结构工整和音韵美，词语或者语义的重复常作为语篇衔接手段，满足表达的美学需要。英文重形合，讲究表达的简洁精炼和用词的多样性。在一般情况下，英语中要避免词语重复，多依靠代词、同义词替换等手段进行语篇衔接，使用重复一般是为了在修辞上起强调作用。因此，在汉英翻译的过程中，需要注意词语的重复问题，进行一定取舍和调整，以使译文在传达源语言意义的同时符合目的语的表达习惯和需要。

25.1 显性重复

显性重复是指在语篇中对某些词语的直接重复使用，或者不同词语在语义上的重复表达，这些重复是明显的、外在的，在翻译时一般可以采取省略、合并或同义词替换等方式进行处理。

[例·真题] 凭着自己对社会现实的理解与感悟，对美好生活的追求与向往，把自己的亲身感受与体验，忠实地记录在岩石之上，同时也为后人留下了神秘瑰丽的贺兰山岩画。

译文 Ancient rock painters faithfully recorded on the rocks their perceptions of social realities and aspirations for a better life as well as their personal experience, which has turned into mysterious, magnificent rock paintings we see today.

分析 这句话使用了多对语义重复的词语，增强了文本韵律美、节奏美和形式美。"理解"和"感悟""追求"和"向往""感受"和"体验"虽然用词不同，但意义相同。由于英文强调语义的简明清楚，要避免重复，因此译文采用删减的方法，仅分别保留一种意义，译为perceptions、aspirations 和 experience。

25.2 隐性重复

隐性重复是指语篇中的某些词语不是词汇外形或语义上的直接重复，但是相互之间存在某种潜在的或者隐性的语义关联。从汉语形式上很难看出来这种重复。汉译英时需要先区分出重复，确定其功能，然后按照显性重复的方法进行处理。

[例·真题] 中国的对外援助，发展巩固了与广大发展中国家的友好关系和经贸合作，推动了南南合作，为人类社会共同发展做出了积极贡献。

译文 Through foreign aid, China has consolidated its friendship and economic and trade cooperation with other developing countries, promoted the South-South cooperation, and contributed to the common development of human society.

分析 这句话中一共出现了三处重复。首先,"发展巩固"在这里强调的是同一意思,属于显性重复,可以合并翻译为 consolidate。其次,"广大"和"发展中国家"两者属于隐性重复,在意义上有潜在关联。发展中国家不止一个,是广泛存在的。这里的"发展中国家"指的是除中国以外所有的发展中国家,其中已经包含了"广大"的意思。所以在翻译时不用再译出"广大"的意思。最后,"积极"和"贡献"也存在潜在的语义关联。"贡献"一词带有感性色彩,属于褒义词,在中文中不存在"不积极的贡献"这种表达,所以不必再重复强调"积极",在翻译时也可省略。

26　四字结构

四字结构是指汉语中由四个汉字构成的短语,包括可随意拆散组合的自由词组,也包括一些固定词组,即成语。从语法关系上来看,汉语四字结构可分为主谓、动宾、偏正和并列关系;而从语义和语用的角度看,它常常在语义表达上或并列或修饰或递进或对比等。相比于寓意丰富、言辞华美的汉语四字结构,英语中更多的是表意清晰、逻辑简明的形合结构,因此在汉译英过程中的翻译方式可以根据具体语境来判断。常见的翻译四字结构的方法有直译法、意译法、省译法等。

26.1　直　译

采用直译法的前提是直译后的英语译文与汉语四字格在所指意义、内涵意义和其他意义上完全相同或对等,且译文符合译入语规范,不会造成误解或引起错误联想。

[例·真题] 中国的对外援助坚持平等互利,注重实效,与时俱进,不附带任何政治条件,形成了具有自身特色的模式。

译文 China's foreign aid endeavors have distinctive Chinese features, as China offers foreign aid on the basis of equality and mutual benefit and in ways are result-oriented, advance with the times and have no political strings attached.

26.2　意　译

由于语言和文化差异,有些四字格,尤其是本身包含独特语言文化形象的四字格,往往无法采用直译法处理,如生灵涂炭、相得益彰、噤若寒蝉、争分夺秒等。这时,只能"牺牲"成语的形象,转而译出其所包含的内涵意义。

[例·真题] 风调雨顺已被视为"奢侈品"。这样的情况下,未雨绸缪才能处变不惊。

译文 With favorable weather now seen as a "luxury", preparedness is essential to building resilient communities.

分析 在这句话中,四字结构"风调雨顺""未雨绸缪"和"处变不惊"属于具有中华文化特色的词汇,很难用直译的方式译出,故而采用意译法,译出词语的含义即可。"风调雨顺"指良好的天气,可以译为 favorable weather。"未雨绸缪"指趁着没下雨先修缮房屋,比喻事先做好准备。"处变不惊"指处在变乱之中,能沉着应对,毫不惊慌。此处结合上下文语意,在雨没来之时做好谋划,建好住所,才能够保持沉着冷静,即"在下雨之前建好房屋是十分重要的",因此可以将该分句译为 preparedness is essential to building resilient communities。

26.3 省 译

汉语四字格往往由两部分组成,呈现多样化的语意关系,如主谓关系、动宾关系等。其中有一类为前后两部分语义重复或同义反复,如三心二意、愁眉苦脸、字斟句酌、招商引资等。处理这类四字格一般采用部分省译法,即不译并列重复的部分,保留四字格的基本意义即可。

[例·真题]岩画<u>造型粗狂稚拙</u>、<u>构图朴实自然</u>,牛、马、驴、鹿、鸟、虎等动物<u>栩栩如生</u>,各种人头的造型同样是<u>千奇百态</u>。

译文 These rock paintings are <u>plain and simple</u> in shape and style, featuring <u>lifelike</u> images of cows, horses, donkeys, deer, brids and tigers and <u>diversified</u> shapes of human heads.

分析 在这句话中,"造型粗狂稚拙""构图朴实自然"两组短语词意相近,本质上都是说岩画不加修饰、简单朴素,因此在翻译时可以不追求字对字的直译,而是选择省译,将语意合并,同时略去冗长的修饰,让译文更加简洁明了,即 plain and simple;"栩栩如生"则是用意译的方法,译为 lifelike;"千奇百态"则属于前后语义重复的四字格,"千"和"百"相对应,"奇"和"态"相对应,可以采用省译法,译为 diversified。

27　隐　喻

　　隐喻是建立在两个意义反映现象之间的某种相似基础上的引申方式。作为一种修辞手法，隐喻用一种事物来比喻另一种事物、行为或特点。隐喻由三部分组成，即主体（比喻对象）、喻体（比喻用语）和喻义（主体和喻体间的相似之处）。尽管使用隐喻会使语言表达更为生动形象，但由于汉英两种语言在文化背景、观念习俗、历史传承、表达习惯等各方面存在差异，翻译隐喻时要采取多种灵活的办法，将目的语包含的深层文化内涵考虑在内，使其符合受众的语言表达习惯和文化语境。

　　英国翻译理论家彼得·纽马克（Peter Newmark）提出了七种隐喻的翻译方法：①直译保留原文意象；②明喻＋释义；③同一隐喻加释义；④用标准的目的语意象代替原文意象；⑤用明喻翻译隐喻；⑥将明喻转为释义；⑦删除隐喻不译。因此，我们将隐喻的译法归为以下五种：直译、归化、异化、转换和释义。

27.1　直　译

　　直译是指在翻译中保留原文的词汇含义和修辞含义。当汉语隐喻中的喻体与英语隐喻中的喻体几乎能够对等，且喻义非常接近时，采取直译方法便可使表达一步到位、易于理解。这相当于纽马克提到的第一种隐喻翻译方法。

[例·真题] 岩画堪称是记载人类早期社会生活的百科全书。

译文 Rock paintings are said to be an encyclopedia that documents the early days of human society.

分析 汉语原句中的"百科全书"，译为英语中的 encyclopedia，恰好能表达岩画作为"百科全书"的内涵概念，所以保留原文修辞，采取直译的方法进行翻译。

27.2　归　化

　　归化是指在翻译中用目的语言的表达习惯和方式传达原文信息，即向目的语读者靠近。如果中文里的隐喻在英文中有对应的俗语表达，则可采取归化的策略，既能使译文既和喻体对应，又能最大化保留原句的文化特色和语言风格。这对应着纽马克提到的第四种隐喻翻译方法。

[例·真题] 美国科罗拉多州等西部地区山火连绵不绝，各地骄阳似火、道路开裂、民众叫苦。

译文 Western parts of America, including Colorado, have been in the midst of incessant wildfires, scorching heat and road cracks, thus resulting in a miserable life for the people.

分析 "骄阳似火"形容太阳像熊熊燃烧的火焰一样炙热,英语中有对应的习惯表达 scorching heat,因此,此处采取归化的翻译方法,使译文更为地道。

[例·真题] 山中无老虎,猴子称大王。

译文 When the cat is not home, the mice dance on the table.

分析 这句话是一个俗语,比喻没有出色的人,差一些的人就能充当主要角色。英文中也有一句俗语表达同样的意思,只不过与例子中的说法不同。因此,采取归化的方法,译为英文中意思相同的俗语,以使目的语读者更好地理解原文意思。

27.3 异化

异化是指在翻译时按照源语言的表达习惯和方式来传达原文信息,即向原文作者靠近,保留源语言的异国风味。在翻译过程中,使用归化策略可能会丧失源语言的文化特色,那么在这种情况下,可以采取异化策略,并进一步解释说明。这也是纽马克提到的第三种隐喻翻译方法。

[例·真题] 在这个意义上,G20 本身就是一座桥,一座连接历史与未来、发达国家与发展中国家的桥梁。

译文 In this sense, G20 itself is a bridge, one that connects history with the future, developed countries with developing ones.

分析 本句中"桥"有着隐喻色彩,且全篇都提到了 G20 峰会的会标是一座桥。因此,这里采取异化的方法,保留原文说法,并将后一句话转换为同位语定语从句对其进行解释说明。

27.4 转换(转明喻)

明喻,是喻体、本体、比喻词同时出现的比喻,是将具有某种共同特征的两种基本上不相同事物连接起来的一种修辞手法。将隐喻添加比喻词,转换为明喻,既可以保留语言中的喻体和形象,又可以准确表达原文信息。

[例·真题] 风调雨顺已被视为"奢侈品"。

译文 Good weather for the crops is just like a luxury.

分析 "奢侈品"是隐喻,原意是指一种超出人们生存与发展需要范围的,具有独特、稀缺、珍奇等特点的消费品,此处添加 like 将汉语隐喻转译为英语句子中的明喻,更能体现原意:风调雨顺的现象和奢侈品一样是很稀缺珍贵的。同时,译文也做到了意思相近、句式相同。

27.5 释　义

释义是指舍弃原文中的具体形象，直接解释原文的意思。在翻译含有隐喻的词语时，如果直译不能使译入语读者明白意思，而加注又使译文太啰嗦，并且原文重意不重形、重意不重典时，可采用释义法。它既可使原文简洁流畅，又不损害对原文信息的传达。

[例·真题] 事实上，人类正处于极端天气的适应期，炎热的酷暑、狂暴的飓风、刺骨的严寒以及滔天的洪水近乎成了"常客"。

译文 Humankind is currently adapting to extreme weather patterns, as evidenced by the common occurrence of horrendous heat waves, ferocious hurricanes, icy cold, and floods from giant deluges.

分析 "常客"原指熟客，常来的宾客，在该语境下指的是经常发生的天气事件。如果将其译为regular customer，很显然不符合该语境传达的意义，会使译文变得晦涩奇怪。因此采取释义的方法，将其译为common occurence，直接解释"常客"在该语境下的意义。

[例·真题] 这个小伙子奉行"宁为玉碎，不为瓦全"的原则。

译文 This young man's principle is "better die in glory than live in dishonor".

分析 汉语善用俗语。本句中的俗语"宁为玉碎，不为瓦全"本意是指宁可为正义的事业献出生命，也不愿丧失气节，苟且偷生。如果直译，则会造成目的语读者的理解障碍。若要采取归化的策略，英文中又没有对应的俗语。所以采取释义法，将其译为better die in glory than live in dishonor。这种译法虽未将汉语原句中"玉""瓦"的形象保留下来，但却传达了与原文相近的信息。

28 特殊句式

汉语有"是"字句、"把"字句、"得"字句等句型,翻译这类句式时没有固定公式或者完全对应的句型,需要根据上下文进行灵活翻译。由于汉语中"把"字句的使用频率较高,接下来以"把"字句为例进行讲解。

"把"字句是通过介词"把"(或"将")将动词支配或影响的对象置于动词之前,使之与动词之间形成动宾关系,因此从意义和作用上来讲,"把"字句是主动句,表达对人或物如何处置的概念。其常见的处理方式有以下五种。

28.1 处置"把"

具有处置意义的"把"字句的谓语动词往往带有状语、补语等成分。在翻译时,可以套用"动词+宾语+补语"或"动词+宾语+介词短语"这两种结构,同时还要注意是否需要根据英文表达习惯将主动句转为被动句。

[例·真题] 中国把"尊重和保障人权"写进了宪法。

译文 Respect for and protection of human rights has been enshrined into the Constitution.

分析 "把……当作/视作/作为"这类句式结构通常表达"看作""视为""认为"等含义,在翻译时可以套用"动词+宾语+as/for"这一英语句型,同时还要注意根据不同的语境选择不同的动词形态(原形或是分词等)。常见的动词有 suppose、treat、mistaken、consider、regard、look、view、take、serve、guide 等。

28.2 把……作为

[例·真题] 北京将把全面治理行人及非机动车交通违法行为作为交通秩序整治的重点。

译文 The municipal government of Beijing vows to overhaul traffic malpractices and irregularities, treated the wrongdoing of pedestrians and non-motor vehicles as the priorities.

28.3 祈使"把"

祈使"把",顾名思义,就是具有祈使意义的"把"字句。这类"把"字句通常是零主语或是无主语,在翻译时可以套用"及物动词+宾语"的英文祈使句句型。

[例] 请把作业按时交上来。

译文 Please hand in your homework on time.

28.4 双宾"把"

双宾"把"即带有双宾语的"把"字句。在翻译此类中文句式时,根据英文的表达习惯,可以将"把"字省略,套用"主语+动词+直接宾语+介词+间接宾语"或"主语+谓语+间接宾语+直接宾语"的英文句型。

[例] 请把锤子递给我。

译文 Please pass me the hammer.

28.5 致使"把"

致使"把"是指含有致使意义的"把"字句。在汉语中,碰到"把"字句中的宾语后加了"气""急""热""迷"等动词,再加"得",再加上表示结果的补语时,通常就是具有了致使意味的句子。在翻译时并没有完全对等的英文句式,需要根据语境以及英文表达习惯选取合适的具有"致使"含义的动词或动词词组。

[例] 外边 40℃的天气把游客们热得都逛不下去了。

译文 It is so hot outside at 40 ℃ that travelers don't want to stroll around anymore.

结论篇

29 "主干定状说"的本质

通过本书前面的讲解,相信大家对于"主干定状说"体系已经较为熟悉。究其本质,便是将所有的中英文句子中的各部分拆解为主干、定语和状语,再进行翻译。

29.1 英译中

[例·真题] A 2010 study in the journal *Social Psychological and Personality Science* found that the percentage of college students exhibiting narcissistic personality traits, based on their scores on the Narcissistic Personality Inventory, a widely used diagnostic test, has increased by more than half since the early 1980s, to 30 percent.

译文 "自恋性格量表"(Narcissistic Personality Inventory)是一种广为使用的诊断测试。2010年,《社会心理学和个性科学》(*Social Psychological and Personality Science*)杂志的一项调查显示,基于该测试分数,自恋性格特点的大学生比例已经增至30%,相比20世纪80年代上涨了50%。

分析 首先提取主干和修饰部分。句子的主干:a study found that…。宾语从句的主干:the percentage has increased。修饰部分:定语,2010、in journal *Social Psychological and Personality Science*、exhibiting narcissistic personality traits;插入语,based on their scores on the Narcissistic Personality Inventory;同位语,a widely used diagnostic test;解释性状语,by more than half、to 30 percent;时间状语,since the early 1980s。其次进行句型解析。定状互换:第一处定语处理为状语,即"2010年",后两处定语均进行前置处理;时间状语处理为定语,修饰 the percentage;插入语处理为状语,即"基于……";由于句式结构复杂,可以将同位语处理为主谓句。

29.2 中译英

[例·真题] 早在1996年,中国就启动实施了"绿色照明工程",中国绿色照明工程的实施,推动了照明电器行业结构的优化升级和产品质量的整体提升,经过多年努力,中国节能灯产品质量水平日益提高,一些企业产品质量和工艺水平已达到世界领先水平。

译文 The initiation of the "Green Lighting Project" which was launched as early as

1996 in our country has improved the industrial structure and the product quality. As a result, the quality of China's energy-saving lamps has been increasingly advanced through years of efforts, with quality and workmanship of some enterprises' products ranking among the best in the world.

分析 由于句子过长,该句可以拆分为两个小句子。分别提取其主干:"绿色照明工程"的实施推动了结构升级和质量提升;质量水平提高。修饰部分:时间状语,早在1996年;地点状语,在中国;定语,中国就启动实施了"绿色照明工程"、中国节能灯产品;方式状语,经过多年努力;解释性状语,一些企业产品质量和工艺水平已达到世界领先水平。再进行句型解析。逻辑关系:因果关系。转译:原文中的动词"实施"译为名词形式。

上述两个长难句翻译思路的分析再次体现了中英文的差异,印证了"主干定状说"的实操价值,反复证明了英译中的本质是处理好定语和状语,汉译英的本质是抓住内在逻辑,将各个成分处理成定语和状语。

经典实战
真题讲解篇

30 2017年5月二级笔译实务真题

30.1 English-Chinese Translation

30.1.1 Passage 1

A ①This agenda is a plan of action for people, the planet and prosperity. ②**It seeks to strengthen universal peace and larger freedom.** ③We recognize that eradicating poverty in all its forms and dimensions is the greatest global challenge and an indispensable requirement for sustainable development. ④We are resolved to free the human race from poverty and heal and protect our planet. ⑤**We are determined to take bold and transformative steps which are urgently needed to shift the world onto a sustainable and resilient path.** ⑥The 17 sustainable development goals and 169 targets which we are announcing today demonstrate the scale and ambition of this new global agenda. ⑦They seek to realize the human rights of all and to achieve gender equality and empowerment of all women and girls. ⑧They are integrated and indivisible and balance the three dimensions of sustainable development: the economic, social, and environmental. ⑨The goals will stimulate action over the next 15 years in areas of critical importance for humanity and the planet.

B ①We are meeting at a time of immense challenges to sustainable development. ②Billions of our citizens are denied a life of dignity. ③There are

A ①本议程是为人类、地球与繁荣制订的行动计划。②它还旨在促进世界和平,提高自由水平。③我们认识到,消除一切形式和维度的贫困是世界面临的最大的挑战,也是实现可持续发展必不可少的要求。④我们决心要让人类摆脱贫困,让地球得到修复和保护。⑤我们决心大胆采取亟需的变革手段,让世界走上可持续且具恢复力的道路。⑥我们今天宣布的17个可持续发展目标和169个具体目标展现了此次新全球议程的规模和宏伟理想。⑦这些目标致力于实现人人享有人权,达成性别平等,赋予所有妇女和儿童权利。⑧这些目标环环相扣,不可分割,并兼顾可持续发展的三个方面:经济、社会和环境。⑨在今后15年中,这些目标将促使我们在有关人类和地球的重要领域中开展行动。

B ①在可持续发展面临巨大挑战之际,我们召开了这次会议。②我们有无数的公民无法过上有尊严的生活。③国家内和国家间的不平等现象不断增加。④性别

rising inequalities within and among countries. ④Gender inequality remains a key challenge. ⑤Unemployment is a major concern. ⑥Global health threats, frequent and intense natural disasters, spiraling conflict, violent extremism, terrorism, related humanitarian crises, and forced displacement of people threaten to reverse much of the development progress made in recent decades. ⑦**Natural resource depletion and the adverse impacts of environmental degradation, including desertification, drought, land degradation, freshwater scarcity, and loss of biodiversity, add to and exacerbate the list of challenges which humanity faces.** ⑧Climate change is one of the greatest challenges of our time, and its adverse impacts undermine the ability of all countries to achieve sustainable development. ⑨The survival of many societies and of the biological support systems of the planet are at risk. ⑩**The *Millennium Development Goals* identified some 15 years ago provided an important framework for development, and significant progress has been made in a number of areas.** ⑪But the progress has been uneven, particularly in Africa, least developed countries, landlocked developing countries, and small island developing States. ⑫And some of the *Millennium Development Goals* remain off-track, in particular those related to maternal, newborn and child health and to reproductive health. ⑬**We recommit ourselves to the full realization of all the *Millennium Development Goals*, including the off-track *Millennium Development Goals*, in particular by providing focused and scaled-up assistance to the least developed countries and other countries in special situations, in line with relevant support programs.** ⑭The new agenda builds on the existing *Millennium Development Goals* and seeks to complete what these did not achieve, particularly in reaching the most vulnerable countries.

不平等仍然面临严峻挑战。⑤失业则是一个令人担忧的重要问题。⑥全球健康面临威胁，自然灾害频繁爆发且程度剧烈，冲突不断升级，暴力极端主义、恐怖主义和相关的人道主义危机不断发生，民众被迫流离失所。这些问题使得最近数十年所取得的大量发展成果功亏一篑。⑦自然资源枯竭、环境恶化带来不良影响（包括沙漠化、干旱、土地退化、淡水匮乏和生物多样性丧失），这些都使得人类面临的各种挑战不断增加且日益严重。⑧气候变化是我们这个时代所面临的最大挑战之一，它产生的不利影响削弱了各个国家实现可持续发展的能力。⑨许多社会以及各种地球生物保障系统遭遇生存威胁。⑩《千年发展目标》大约是在15年前制订的，它为发展提供了重要体系框架，并且在一些领域已经取得了重大进展。⑪但是这些发展是不均衡的，非洲、最不发达国家、内陆发展中国家和小岛屿发展中国家尤其如此。⑫一些千年发展目标仍然未达成，特别是那些有关产妇、新生儿及儿童健康的目标，和有关生殖健康的目标。⑬我们再次承诺，我们会全面实现包括尚未达成的千年发展目标在内的所有目标，特别是根据相关支持方案，向最不发达国家和其他处于特殊情形的国家提供有针对性的和全面的帮助。⑭新议程以现有的千年发展目标为基础，旨在完成尚未实现的目标，尤其关注最为脆弱的国家。

重点句子分析

1. It seeks to strengthen universal peace and larger freedom.

第一步　主从分析

主干：It seeks to strengthen universal peace and larger freedom。

第二步　句型解析

A. 代词 it：指代上句中提到的"议程"。

B. 动词的分配原则：句中有一个非谓语动词 to strengthen，peace 和 freedom 为并列成分，作非谓语动词 to strengthen 的宾语。因此，可将 strengthen 分别翻译为"促进"和"提高"，与宾语一一对应。

C. freedom 的处理：增加范畴词"水平"。

D. 逻辑关系：与上句构成递进关系，翻译时加上"还"。

第三步　翻译

它还旨在促进世界和平，提高自由水平。

2. We recognize that eradicating poverty in all its forms and dimensions is the greatest global challenge and an indispensable requirement for sustainable development.

第一步　主从分析

主干：we recognize that… 。

宾语从句主干：eradicating poverty is the challenge and a requirement。

修饰：定语 in all its forms and dimensions（修饰 poverty）、the greatest global（修饰 challenge）、indispensable（修饰 requirement）、for sustainable development（修饰 requirement）。

第二步　句型解析

A. 宾语从句长，单独处理。

B. dimensions 的处理：译为"表现"。

C. 增加动词：challenge 译为"面临的挑战"；requirement 译为"实现……的要求"。

第三步　翻译

我们认识到，消除一切形式和维度的贫困是世界面临的最大挑战，也是实现可持续发展必不可少的要求。

3. We are determined to take bold and transformative steps which are urgently needed to shift the world onto a sustainable and resilient path.

第一步　主从分析

主干：we are determined to take steps。

修饰：定语1 bold and transformative,修饰 steps;定语2 which are urgently needed,修饰 steps;目的状语 to shift the world onto a sustainable and resilient path,修饰 are determined。

第二步　句型解析

A. 定语1 的处理：定状互换,译为"大胆采取"。

B. 定语2 的处理：两种处理方式,第一种前置处理为"迫切需要的;亟需的";第二种后置单独处理。

第三步　翻译

A. 我们决心大胆采取迫切需要的变革步骤,让世界走上可持续且具有恢复力的道路。

B. 我们决心大胆采取变革步骤,这些步骤是迫切需要的,用这种方式让世界走上可持续且具有恢复力的道路。

4. Natural resource depletion and the adverse impacts of environmental degradation, including desertification, drought, land degradation, freshwater scarcity and loss of biodiversity, add to and exacerbate the list of challenges which humanity faces.

第一步　主从分析

主干：natural resource depletion and the adverse impacts add to and exacerbate the list of challenges。

修饰：插入语 including desertification, drought, land degradation, freshwater scarcity and loss of biodiversity,补充说明 impacts;定语 of environmental degradation（修饰 impacts）、which humanity faces（修饰 challenges）。

第二步　句型解析

A. 主语长,单独处理。

B. 插入语的处理：译为主谓结构。

C. exacerbate 的处理：转译为"(使得……)日益严重"。

第三步　翻译

自然资源枯竭、环境恶化带来不良影响(包括沙漠化、干旱、土地退化、淡水匮乏和生物多样性丧失),这些都使得人类面临的各种挑战不断增加且日益严重。

5. The *Millennium Development Goals* identified some 15 years ago provided an important framework for development, and significant progress has been made in a number of areas.

第一步 主从分析

主干：the *Millennium Development Goals* provided an important framework, and progress has been made。

修饰：定语 identified some 15 years ago（修饰 the *Millennium Development Goals*）、for development（修饰 framework）；地点状语 in a number of areas，修饰 has been made。

第二步 句型解析

A. 定语 identified some 15 years ago 的处理：有非谓语动词，后置处理为主谓结构，即"大约是在15年前制订的"。

B. 被动变主动：significant progress has been made 译为"取得重大进展"。

第三步 翻译

《千年发展目标》大约是在15年前制订的，它为发展提供了重要框架，并且在一些领域已经取得了重大进展。

6. We recommit ourselves to the full realization of all the *Millennium Development Goals*, including the off-track *Millennium Development Goals*, in particular by providing focused and scaled-up assistance to the least developed countries and other countries in special situations, in line with relevant support programs.

第一步 主从分析

主干：we recommit ourselves to the full realization。

修饰：定语 of all the Millennium Development Goals，修饰 realization；插入语 including the off-track Millennium Development Goals，补充说明 goals；方式状语 in particular by providing focused and scaled-up assistance to the least developed countries and other countries in special situations（修饰 recommit）、in line with relevant support programs（修饰 providing）。

第二步 句型解析

A. 抽象名词 realization 的处理：译为动词"实现"。

B. full 的处理：定语状语互换，译为"全面"。

C. 方式状语的处理：前置翻译。

D. focused and scaled-up 的处理：译为"有针对性的和全面的"。

第三步 翻译

我们再次承诺，我们会全面实现包括尚未达成的千年发展目标在内的所有目标，特别是根据相关支持方案，向最不发达国家和其他处于特殊情形的国家提供有针对性的和全面的帮助。

30.1.2　Passage 2

A　①Entrepreneurs in Silicon Valley, only half-jokingly, call it the URL strategy. ②The three letters usually stand for Uniform Resource Locator—the unique address of any file that is accessible via the Internet. ③But in the world of Internet start-ups, URL has another meaning: ubiquity first, revenue later. ④**This pretty much describes the strategy of most big online social networks, which over the past few years have concentrated on increasing users rather than worrying about profits.** ⑤That has allowed them to build huge followings, but it has also raised a big question over their ability to make money from the audiences they have put together. ⑥**The issue is whether the social-networking industry can come up with a successful form of advertising that enables it to succeed in the same way that Google has been able to make billions of dollars from the targeted ads that run alongside the search results.** ⑦Without such a formula, runs the argument, social networks such as Facebook will never amount to much. ⑧Doubters claim that the networks face two big handicaps. ⑨The first is that people log into social-networking sites to hang out with their friends, so they will pay no attention to ads. ⑩**The second is that because the sites let users generate their own content, they will find it hard to attract advertisers because brands will not want to take the risk of appearing alongside examples of profanity, obscenity or nudity-or all three at once.**

B　①But the broader outlook for networking sites is more encouraging. ②One reason is that advertisers are being drawn to the leading sites by their sheer scale. ③Facebook's audience is bigger than any TV network that has ever existed on the face of the earth. ④**And the networks can target ads with laser-like precision, thanks to the data they hold on their users' ages, gender, interests, and so forth.** ⑤Although there are still lingering concerns about brands appearing next to racy content, firms seem more willing to run this risk now that the networks' advertising proposition has increased. ⑥Aside from the advertising-driven business model, some are also making healthy profits from sales of games and virtual goods. ⑦The beauty of this business for social networks is that the cost of producing and storing virtual inventory is minimal. ⑧Moreover, because these are closed markets, networks can fix prices at levels that generate huge profits. ⑨**To some, the notion that big money can be made from selling make-believe items may seem bizarre, but the practice replicates physical presents that people give to one another to cement relationships in the real world.**

任何电视观众的数量都多。④并且，得益于社交网络掌握的大量用户数据，包括年龄、性别、兴趣，社交网络投放广告如激光般精确，这也是广告公司青睐的一点。⑤尽管广告公司依然会担心商品会和不雅内容一起出现，但广告公司现在更愿意冒这个风险，原因在于社交网络的广告策划越来越多。⑥除了广告驱动的商业模型，还有一些社交网络公司也通过出售游戏和虚拟产品挣到了不菲收益。⑦此类交易的迷人之处在于生产和储存虚拟产品的成本非常低。⑧另外，由于这些都是封闭市场，网络可以将价格抬高从而获取巨额收益。⑨对一些人来说，以售卖虚拟产品赚大钱的想法似乎十分怪异，但这和现实世界中人们互送实体礼物拉近关系的做法十分接近。

重点句子分析

1. This pretty much describes the strategy of most big online social networks, which over the past few years have concentrated on increasing users rather than worrying about profits.

第一步　主从分析

主干：this describes the strategy。

修饰：定语 of most big online social networks, 修饰 strategy；非限制性定语从句 which over the past few years have concentrated on increasing users rather than worrying about profits。

第二步　句型解析

A. this 的指代：指代上文的 URL，译为"该词语"。

B. 定语从句的处理：句子较长，后置单独处理。

C. 抽象名词的处理：strategy 抽象名词增加动词，翻译成"所采取的策略"。

第三步　翻译

该词语很精确地概括了绝大多数大型在线社交网络公司所采取的策略,这类公司在过去的数年专注于积累用户,对盈利倒不是很关心。

2. The issue is whether the social-networking industry can come up with a successful form of advertising that enables it to succeed in the same way that Google has been able to make billions of dollars from the targeted ads that run alongside the search results.

第一步　主从分析

主干:the issue is whether the social-networking industry can come up with a successful form of advertising。

修饰:定语 that enables it to succeed(修饰 advertising)、that run alongside the search results(修饰 ads);方式状语 in the same way;同位语 that Google has been able to make billions of dollars from the targeted ads,修饰 way。

第二步　句型解析

A. 定语1的处理:偏正结构处理成动宾结构。

B. 定语2的处理:前置处理为"伴随搜索结果运营的"。

C. 同位语的处理:处理为主谓结构。

第三步　翻译

问题就是社交网络产业能否推出一个成功的广告模式,一个能够使该行业如同谷歌那样取得成功的广告模式——谷歌能根据搜索结果,精准投放广告,已经从中盈利数十亿美元。

3. The second is that because the sites let users generate their own content, they will find it hard to attract advertisers because brands will not want to take the risk of appearing alongside examples of profanity, obscenity or nudity-or all three at once.

第一步　主从分析

主干:the second is that…。

修饰:主语补足语 they will find it hard to attract advertisers;原因状语从句 because the sites let users generate their own content、because brands will not want to take the risk of…；形式宾语 it;定语 of appearing alongside examples(修饰 risk)、of profanity, obscenity, or nudity(修饰 examples)。

第二步　句型解析

A. 反话正说:the sites let users generate their own content 翻译成"用户自主生成网页内容"。

B. 第二处原因状语的处理:单独处理,放在结尾。

第三步　翻译

其二，由于网站用户发表内容自由，广告主们则很难被吸引，因为投放的广告可能会出现在一些亵渎言论、猥亵字眼或裸露镜头旁边——甚至可能三者同时出现，他们不想冒这个险。

4. And the networks can target ads with laser-like precision, thanks to the data they hold on their users ages, gender, interests, and so forth.

第一步　主从分析

主干：The networks can target ads。

修饰：修饰性状语 with laser-like precision，修饰 can target；原因状语 thanks to the data they hold on their users ages, gender, interests, and so forth，修饰 can target；定语 they hold on their users ages, genders, interests, and so forth，修饰 the data。

第二步　句型解析

A. 原因状语的处理：就整个句子而言，先翻译原因状语。

B. 定语的处理：偏正结构处理成主谓结构，译为"掌握大量用户数据，包括年龄、性别、兴趣"。

C. 修饰性状语的处理：修饰动词。

第三步　翻译

并且，得益于社交网络掌握大量用户数据，包括年龄、性别、兴趣，社交网络投放广告如激光般精确，这也是广告公司青睐的一点。

5. To some, the notion that big money can be made from selling make-believe items may seem bizarre, but the practice replicates physical presents that people give to one another to cement relationships in the real world.

第一步　主从分析

主干：the notion may seem bizarre, but the practice replicates physical presents。

修饰：同位语 that big money can be made from selling make-believe items，修饰 notion；定语 that people give to one another，修饰 presents。

第二步　句型解析

A. 同位语的处理：处理成定语，译为"以售卖虚拟产品赚大钱的做法"。

B. replicates 的处理：本意为"复制"，这里应该指这种做法和实体礼物的作用相似；为了语序自然，replicates 单独处理，放在句尾。

C. 定语的处理：偏正结构处理成动宾结构，physical presents that people give to one another 译为"互送"。

第三步　翻译

对一些人来说，以售卖虚拟产品赚大钱的想法似乎十分怪异，但这和现实世界中人们互送实体礼物拉近关系的做法十分接近。

30.2 Chinese-English Translation

30.2.1 Passage 1

A ①本公司是全球最大最强的冶金建设运营服务商。②拥有24万在职员工,资产规模超7000亿元,境外机构资源项目与承建工程遍布全球60多个国家和地区。③本公司有着独特的全产业链竞争优势,在全球金属矿业领域率先打通了从资源获取勘查、设计施工、运营到流通、深加工的全产业链,形成了为金属矿产企业提供系统性解决方案和工程建设运营一体化全生命周期的服务能力。

B ①本公司金属矿产资源储量丰富,在国内外拥有一批世界级优质矿山。②在冶金工业建设领域,公司积累了贯穿各环节的核心技术优势和设计施工能力,承担了中国大中型钢铁企业超过90%的设计施工任务和全球60%冶金建设任务,是冶金建设的"国家队"。③公司拥有遍布全球的贸易流通网络。全球采购、全球营销,金属矿产品流通规模稳居国内第一。

A ①Our corporation is the world's largest and strongest service provider for the development and operation of the metallurgical industry. ②It has 240,000 employees, assets worth 700 billion yuan, and overseas subsidiaries, resource and construction projects in over 60 countries and regions. ③The company has unique competitive advantages across the full industrial chain. It becomes the first company in the global metal industry to establish presence in the full industrial chain from resource acquisition, investigation, design, construction, operation to logistics and deep processing; capable of providing systematic solutions and integrated life cycle services covering engineering, construction and operation to other metal mining companies.

B ①The company owns abundant reserves of metals, with many world-class top-quality mines at home and abroad. ②In the metallurgical engineering industry, the company has core technologies in every process and strong capabilities in designing and construction. As a state-owned enterprise for China's metallurgical industry, it has undertaken more than 90 percent of the designing and construction jobs of large and medium-sized iron and steel enterprises in China and 60 percent of the metallurgical construction projects around the world. ③In addition, it has a global trade network for procurement and marketing and ranks the first in China in terms of the distribution volume of metal ore products.

重点句子分析

1. 本公司有着独特的全产业链竞争优势,在全球金属矿业领域率先打通了从资源获取、勘查、设计施工、运营到流通、深加工的全产业链,形成了为金属矿产企业提供系统性解决方案和工程建设运营一体化全生命周期的服务能力。

第一步　主从分析

主干:本公司有着竞争优势,打通了全产业链,形成了服务能力。

修饰:地点状语"在全球金属矿业领域";评注性状语"率先";定语"独特的全产业链""从资源获取、勘查、设计施工、运营到流通、深加工的""系统性""工程建设运营一体化全生命周期的";宾语补足语"为金属矿产企业"。

第二步　句型解析

A. 结构的划分:整句由于有过多的定状成分,需要切分成两个句子,成为总—分的结构。第一个句子中有主语"本公司",第二个句子需要添加主语,用 it 代替。

B. 定语"工程建设运营一体化全生命周期的"的处理:较长,作后置定语。

C. 评注性状语的处理:"率先"定状互换,译为定语 first。

第三步　翻译

The company has unique competitive advantages across the full industrial chain. It becomes the first company in the global metal industry to establish presence in the full industrial chain from resource acquisition, investigation, design, construction, operation to logistics and deep processing; and it is capable of providing systematic solutions and integrated life cycle services covering engineering, construction and operation to other mental mining companies.

2. 本公司金属矿产资源储量丰富,在国内外拥有一批世界级优质矿山。

第一步　主从分析

主干:本公司(拥有)金属矿产资源。

修饰:定语"储量丰富";伴随状语"在国内外拥有一批世界级优质矿山"。

第二步　句型解析

A. 名词的选择:"金属矿产资源"就是 metals;"储量"用 reserves,都要注意加"s"。

B. 逻辑关系:英文先说结论,后说事实,本句处理为主从关系。

第三步　翻译

The company owns abundant reserves of metals, with many world-class top-quality mines at home and abroad.

30.2.2　Passage 2

A　①我们要积极推进结构性改革尤其是供给侧结构性改革。②**中国经济发展面临的结构性矛盾,供给和需求两侧都有,主要在供给侧。**③我们要用改革的办法推进结构调整,减少无效和低端的供给,扩大有效和中高端的供给。④这既有利于经济转型,也有利于促进增长。

B　①其中很重要的就是要淘汰落后产能,化解过剩产能,重点是抓好钢铁、煤炭等困难行业去产能。②这方面近几年已取得初步成效,原煤、粗钢产量减少,但还要继续加以推动,主要是通过运用市场化、法治化手段,严格环保、质量、安全等标准。③去产能最大的难题是人往哪里去。④企业要采取多种措施使职工转岗不下岗,中央和地方政府都要对职工分流安置给予必要的支持。⑤产能过剩是一个全球性的问题,我们主动采取行动去产能,说明中国是负责任的国家。

A　①We need to push forward structural reform, especially supply-side reform. ②The structural problems facing the Chinese economy are about both the supply and demand sides, especially the supply side. ③We will facilitate structural adjustment through reform, reduce inefficient and low-end supply, and expand effective and medium- and high-end supply. ④This is conducive to economic transformation as well as growth.

B　①A major task for us is to phase out outdated production capacity and address/resolve overcapacity, with a focus on steel, coal and other sectors that face difficulty. ②Recent years we have witnessed some initial progress, such as the reduced production of raw coal and crude steel. But there remains much to be done. We will strictly enforce standards in environmental protection, quality and safety by leveraging the role of the market and law. ③The biggest challenge in cutting overcapacity is how to address displaced workers. ④Businesses need to take multiple measures to ensure that their employees will get reemployed. Both the central and local governments should provide necessary support to take care of the affected employees. ⑤Overcapacity is a global challenge. We have taken the initiative to cut overcapacity, which demonstrates that China is indeed a responsible country.

重点句子分析

1. 中国经济发展面临的结构性矛盾,供给和需求两侧都有,主要在供给侧。

第一步　主从分析

主干:结构性矛盾供给和需求两侧都有。
修饰:定语"中国经济发展面临的";评注性状语"主要在供给侧"。

第二步　句型解析

A. 定语的处理：定语较长，后置翻译，译为 facing the Chinese economy。

B. 评注性状语的处理：与主句用逗号隔开。

C. 确定关键名词：结构性矛盾 structural problems/contradictions。

第三步　翻译

The structural problems facing the Chinese economy are about both the supply and demand sides, especially the supply side.

2. 其中很重要的就是要淘汰落后产能，化解过剩产能；重点是抓好钢铁、煤炭等困难行业去产能。

第一步　主从分析

主干：其中很重要的是淘汰产能，化解产能。

修饰：评注性状语"重点是抓好钢铁、煤炭等困难行业去产能"；定语"落后""过剩"。

第二步　句型解析

A. 中文句子缺少主语，翻译成英语要添加主语。

B. 评注性状语的处理："重点是抓好钢铁、煤炭等困难行业去产能"与上句"化解过剩产能"表达含义相同且为递进的逻辑关系，可考虑合并，用 especially in/with a focus on 连接。

C. 确定关键名词："落后产能"outdated production capacity，"过剩产能"overcapacity。

第三步　翻译

A major task for us is to phase out outdated production capacity and address/resolve overcapacity, with a focus on steel, coal and other sectors that face difficulty.

3. 企业要采取多种措施使职工转岗不下岗，中央和地方政府都要对职工分流安置给予必要的支持。

第一步　主从分析

主干：企业采取措施，政府给予支持。

修饰：定语"多种""中央和地方""必要的"；目的状语"使职工转岗不下岗"；宾语补足语"对职工分流安置"。

第二步　句型解析

A. 明确句意："转岗不下岗"即"下岗后安排另一份工作"译为 employees will get reemployed；"职工分流安置"即"对相关工人进行安置"译为 take care of the affected employees。

B. 逻辑关系：并列关系，且有独立主谓结构，可断为两句。

第三步　翻译

Businesses need to take multiple measures to ensure that their employees will get reemployed. Both the central and local governments should provide necessary support to take care of the affected employees.

31　2019年6月二级笔译实务真题

31.1　English-Chinese Translation

31.1.1　Passage 1

A　①In 2009, *Time* magazine hailed *School of One*, an online math program piloted at three New York City public schools, as one of the year's 50 best innovation. ②**Each day, *School of One* software generated individualized math "playlists" for students who then chose the "modality" in which they wished to learn—software, a virtual teacher or a fresh-and-blood one.** ③A different algorithm sorted teachers' specialties and schedules to match a student's needs. ④"It generates the lessons, the tests and it grades the tests," one veteran instructor marveled. ⑤It saved salaries, too, thereby "teacher proofing" (as policy wonks say) education in a few clicks.

B　①**Although *School of One* made only modest improvements in students' math scores and was adopted by only a handful of New York schools (not the 50 for which it was slated), it serves as a notable example of a pattern that Andrea Gabor, who holds the Bloomberg chair of business journalism at Baruch College/CUNY, charts in *After the Education Wars*.** ②For more than three decades, an unlikely coalition of corporate philanthropists, educational technology entrepreneurs and public education bureaucrats has spearheaded a brand of school reform characterized by the overvaluing of technology and standardized testing

A　①2009年,《时代周刊》赞誉"一校通"为年度50项最佳创新发明之一。该项目是一项在纽约市三所公立学校进行试点的在线数学项目。②"一校通"软件每天都会为学生生成个性化的数学"播放列表",随后学生可以根据喜好选择想要的上课方式,这些方式包括软件授课、虚拟教师和真人教师。③还有另外一种不同的算法,这种算法对老师的专长和课表进行分类,以此来匹配学生的需要。④一位资深教师赞叹道:"这款软件可以生成课程和测试,并给出测试的分数。"⑤该软件还同样节省了薪资支出,有了它,教师们只需要点几下鼠标,就可以实现那些政策研究者所说的"无教师主导"教育。

B　①尽管"一校通"在学生数学成绩提高上收效甚微,且纽约市只有少数几所(而非计划安排的50所)学校实施了该项目,但它是安德莉亚·加博尔(此人是纽约州立大学巴鲁学院彭博商业新闻学的主席)在《教育战争之后》一书中描绘的教育模式的鲜明例证。②三十多年来,企业慈善家、专注于教育技术的企业家和公共教育

and a devaluing of teachers and communities.

C ①The trend can be traced back to a hyperbolic 1983 report, *A Nation at Risk*, issued by President Ronald Reagan's National Commission on Excellence in Education. ②**Against the backdrop of an ascendant Japanese economy and consistent with President Reagan's disdain for public education (and teachers' unions)**, *A Nation at Risk* **blamed America's ineffectual schools for a "rising tide of mediocrity" that was diminishing America's global role in a new high-tech world.**

D ①Policymakers turned their focus to public education as a matter of national security, one too important (and potentially too profitable) to entrust to educators. ②**The notion that top-down decisions by politicians, not teachers, should determine what children need was a thread running through the bi-partisan 2001** *No Child Left Behind Act*, **the Obama administration's Race to the Top and state-initiated Common Core standards, and the current charter-driven agenda of Secretary of Education Betsy DeVos.** ③"Accountability" became synonymous with standardized tests, resulting in a testing juggernaut with large profits going to commercial publishing giants like Pearson.

E ①The education wars have been demoralizing for teachers, over 17 percent of whom drop out within their first five years. ②**No one believes that teaching to the test is good pedagogy, but what are the options when students' future educational choices, teachers' salaries and retention and, in some states, the fate of entire schools rest on student test scores?**

F ①In meticulous if sometimes too laborious detail, Gabor documents reform's institutional failings. ②**She describes the story tuns in New York City's testing-obsessed policies, the undermining of**

官员不可思议地联合起来,共同带头实施了一项学校改革。这项改革的主要特点是过度强调技术和标准化考试而弱化了教师和社会的作用。

C ①这种趋势可追溯至1983年一份言辞夸张的报告,该报告名为《危机中的国家》,由罗纳德·里根总统执政时期的美国国家卓越教育委员会发布。②当时,日本经济不断崛起,而里根总统一向轻视公共教育(以及教师群体),《危机中的国家》与总统的口吻如出一辙,指责正是美国那些教育质量低下的学校造成了美国"日渐蔓延的平庸浪潮",而其也削弱了美国在高科技新时代的国际地位。

D ①政策制定者们将注意力投向公共教育,将其上升到国家安全层面,由于公共教育的意义非常重大(也可能是利润太高),因此不能交托给教育工作者。②有种观点认为,决定儿童需求的应是政客们自上而下的决策,而非教师。从2001年美国两党一致支持的《有教无类法案》,到奥巴马政府宣布的"力争上游"计划,再到"各州共同核心课程标准"和目前教育部部长贝琪·德沃斯提出的特许学校制度,这一理念贯穿始终。③"责任制"已变成标准化测试的同义词,并催生了一个庞大的考试体制,其中产生的大量利润都流入像皮尔森这样的商业出版巨头。

E ①一直以来,教育之战削弱了老师们的士气,超过17%的老师在他们从业五年内辞职转行。②没有人认为应试教育是好的教育方式,但当学生的教育选择、教师的薪资和任职,甚至在某些州,整个学校的命运都取决于学生的考试成绩时,又能做何选择呢?

Michigan's once fine public schools (spurred in part by constant pressure from the DeVos family) and the heart-breaking failure of New Orleans to remake its schools after Hurricane Katrina. ③The largely white city establishment bypassed the majority-black community, inviting philanthropists and the federal government to rebuild its public schools as the nation's first citywide, all-charter system. ④A dozen years later, more than a third of the city's charter schools have failed.

F ①加博尔在这本书中十分细致地，甚至有时过于详尽地记录了教育体制改革的诸多缺陷。②她记载了纽约市以应试为导向的教育政策带来的消极转变，密歇根州几所优秀公立学校的没落（部分原因是由德沃斯家族的持续施压所致），以及新奥尔良市在卡特里娜飓风袭击后重建当地学校的令人心碎的惨状。③以白人为主的城市权力架构置以黑人为主的社群于不顾，邀请慈善家和联邦政府重建当地的公立学校，建成了美国首个覆盖全市的全特许教育体系。④但是，十几年后，该市超过三分之一的特许学校以失败告终。

重点句子分析

1. Each day, *School of One* software generated individualized math "playlists" for students who then chose the "modality" in which they wished to learn—software, a virtual teacher or a fresh-and-blood one.

第一步　主从分析

主干：*School of One* software generated individualized math "playlists"。

修饰：时间状语 each day；定语 for students who then chose the "modality"、in which they wished to learn；同位语 software, a virtual teacher or a fresh-and-blood one。

第二步　句型解析

A. 循环定语的处理：第一处定语与主句存在时间先后的逻辑关系，第二处定语较短，前置处理。上述定语译为"随后学生可以根据喜好选择想要的上课方式"。

B. 同位语的处理：处理为顶针结构，译为"这些方式包括软件授课、虚拟教师和真人教师"。

第三步　翻译

"一校通"软件每天都会为学生生成个性化的数学"播放列表"，随后学生可以根据喜好选择想要的上课方式，这些方式包括软件授课、虚拟教师和真人教师。

2. Although *School of One* **made only modest improvements in students' math scores and was adopted by only a handful of New York schools（not the 50 for which it was slated）, it serves as a notable example of a pattern that Andrea Gabor, who holds the Bloomberg chair of business journalism at Baruch College/CUNY, charts in** *After the Education Wars*.

第一步　主从分析

主干：it serves as a notable example。

修饰：让步状语 although *School of One* made only modest improvements in students' math scores and was adopted by only a handful of New York schools（not the 50 for which it was slated）；定语 of a pattern that Andrea Gabor charts in *After the Education Wars*、who holds the Bloomberg chair of business journalism at Baruch College/CUNY。

第二步　句型解析

A. 被动变主动：（*School of One*）"was adopted by ... schools"译为"只有几所学校实施了……"。

B. slate 的处理：在此处为"计划；安排"的意思。

C. 第二处定语的处理：定语从句过长，单独成句，在中心词后加（）作补充说明。译为"（此人是纽约州立大学巴鲁学院彭博商业新闻学的主席）"。

第三步　翻译

尽管"一校通"在学生数学成绩提高上收效甚微，且纽约市只有少数几所（而非计划安排的 50 所）学校实施了该项目，但它是安德莉亚·加博尔（此人是纽约州立大学巴鲁学院彭博商业新闻学的主席）在《教育战争之后》一书中描绘的教育模式的鲜明例证。

3. Against the backdrop of an ascendant Japanese economy and consistent with President Reagan's disdain for public education（and teachers' unions）, *A Nation at Risk* **blamed America's ineffectual schools for a "rising tide of mediocrity" that was diminishing America's global role in a new high-tech world.**

第一步　主从分析

主干：*A Nation at Risk* blamed America's ineffectual schools。

修饰：评注性状语 against the backdrop of an ascendant Japanese economy and consistent with President Reagan's disdain for public education（and teachers' unions）；原因状语 for a "rising tide of mediocrity"；定语 that was diminishing America's global role in a new high-tech world。

第二步　句型解析

A. 词性转换：为更符合中文动态语言的表达习惯，名词词组 an ascendant Japanese economy 中，形容词 ascendant 转换为动词"攀升，不断崛起"；consistent with President

Reagan's disdain 中,名词 disdain 转换为动词"轻视,蔑视"。

B. 评注性状语的处理:原句此处省略了 being,此处应按照(being) against the backdrop…and (being) consistent with…的完整表达理解句子,译为"当时,……,而……"。

C. 后置定语的处理:定语较长,单独成句,译为"而其也削弱了美国在高科技新时代的国际地位"。

D. 定状互换:状语 in a new high-tech world 转换为定语,译为"在高科技新时代的"。

E. 增词:增添本位词"其",指代"日渐蔓延的平庸浪潮"。

第三步 翻译

当时,日本经济不断崛起,而里根总统一向轻视公共教育(以及教师群体),《危机中的国家》与总统的口吻如出一辙,指责正是美国那些教育质量低下的学校造成了美国"日渐蔓延的平庸浪潮",而其也削弱了美国在高科技新时代的国际地位。

4. The notion that top-down decisions by politicians, not teachers, should determine what children need was a thread running through the bi-partisan 2001 *No Child Left Behind Act*, the Obama administration's Race to the Top and state-initiated Common Core standards, and the current charter-driven agenda of Secretary of Education Betsy DeVos.

第一步 主从分析

主干:the notion was a thread。

修饰:同位语 that top-down decisions by politicians, not teachers, should determine what children need;后置定语 running through the bi-partisan 2001 *No Child Left Behind Act*, the Obama administration's Race to the Top and state-initiated Common Core standards, and the current charter-driven agenda of Secretary of Education Betsy DeVos。

第二步 句型解析

A. 同位语的处理:处理为主谓结构,译为"决定儿童需求的应是政客们自上而下的决策,而非教师"。

B. 词性转换:将名词 thread 转换为动词短语"贯穿始终"。

C. 定语从句的处理:定语从句较长,单独处理。译为"从 2001 年美国两党一致支持的《有教无类法案》,到奥巴马政府宣布的'力争上游'计划,再到"各州共同核心课程标准"和目前教育部部长贝琪·德沃斯提出的特许学校制度"。

D. 专有名词的处理:*No Child Left Behind Act* 译为《有教无类法案》;Race to the Top 译为"力争上游"计划;state-initiated Common Core standards 译为"各州共同核心课程标准"。

E. 增词:原句过长,在断句时,可将主语 the notion 与其同位语合并成句,增加谓语动词"认为"。

第三步　翻译

有种观点认为,决定儿童需求的应是政客们自上而下的决策,而非教师。从 2001 年美国两党一致支持的《有教无类法案》,到奥巴马政府宣布的"力争上游"计划,再到"各州共同核心课程标准"和目前教育部部长贝琪·德沃斯提出的特许学校制度,这一理念贯穿始终。

5. No one believes that teaching to the test is good pedagogy, but what are the options when students' future educational choices, teachers' salaries and retention and, in some states, the fate of entire schools rest on student test scores?

第一步　主从分析

主干:no one believes that teaching to the test is good pedagogy, but what are the options?

修饰:条件状语 when students' future educational choices, teachers' salaries and retention and, the fate of entire schools rest on student test scores;地点状语 in some states。

第二步　句型解析

A. 状语的处理:条件状语较长,前置单独处理。译为"但是,当学生的教育选择、教师的薪资和任职,甚至在某些州,整个学校的命运都取决于学生的考试成绩时"。

B. 逻辑关系:将条件状语中的 and 译为"甚至",体现递进关系。

第三步　翻译

没有人认为应试教育是好的教育方式,但是,当学生的教育选择、教师的薪资和任职,甚至在某些州,整个学校的命运都取决于学生的考试成绩时,又能做何选择呢?

6. She describes the story turns in New York City's testing-obsessed policies, the undermining of Michigan's once fine public schools (spurred in part by constant pressure from the DeVos family) and the heart-breaking failure of New Orleans to remake its Schools after Hurricane Katrina.

第一步　主从分析

主干:she describes the story turns, the undermining and the failure。

修饰:定语 in New York City's testing-obsessed policies、of Michigan's once fine public schools (spurred in part by constant pressure from the DeVos family)、heart-breaking、of New Orleans to remake its schools;时间状语 after Hurricane Katrina。

第二步　句型解析

A. story 的处理:根据句意及其他两组定语的感情色彩,将其译为"消极的"。

B. 词性转换:将介词短语 in part 转换为名词短语,译为"部分原因"。

C. 定语的处理:第一、第二、第四处均前置处理。分别译为"纽约市以应试为导向的""密歇根州几所优秀公立学校的""新奥尔良市重建当地学校的"。

D. 时间状语的处理:前置,根据句意增词"袭击",译为"在卡特里娜飓风袭击后"。

第三步　翻译

她记载了纽约市以应试为导向的教育政策带来的消极转变,密歇根州几所优秀公立学校的没落(部分原因是由德沃斯家族的持续施压所致),以及新奥尔良市在卡特里娜飓风袭击后重建当地学校的令人心碎的惨状。

31.1.2　Passage 2

A　①Angkor is one of the most important archaeological sites in South-East Asia. ②For several centuries, Angkor, was the centre of the Khmer Kingdom. ③**With impressive monuments, several different ancient urban plans and large water reservoirs, the site is a unique concentration of features testifying to an exceptional civilization.** ④The architecture and layout of the successive capitals bear witness to a high level of social order and ranking within the Khmer Empire. ⑤Angkor is therefore a major site exemplifying cultural, religious and symbolic values, as well as containing high architectural, archaeological and artistic significance.

B　①The park is inhabited, and many villages, in some of whom the ancestors are dating back to the Angkor period, are scattered throughout the park. ②The Angkor complex encompasses all major architectural buildings and hydrological engineering systems from the Khmer period and most of these "barays" and canals still exist today. ③All the individual aspects illustrate the intactness of the site very much reflecting the splendor of the cities that once were. ④**The site integrity however, is put under dual pressures: endogenous, exerted by more than 100,000 inhabitants distributed over 112 historic settlements scattered over the site, who constantly try to expand their dwelling areas; exogenous, related to the proximity of the town of Siem Reap, the seat of the province and a tourism hub.**

A　①吴哥(Angkor)是东南亚地区最为重要的考古遗址之一。②几个世纪以来,吴哥一直是高棉帝国的中心。③吴哥拥有着令人惊叹的历史遗迹、几处古城池以及大型水库遗址,是一个拥有杰出文明且独一无二的特点集中地。④吴哥延绵的建筑与布局见证了高棉帝国高水平的社会地位和秩序。⑤吴哥是一处历史意义重大的遗址,因为它不仅仅彰显出文化、宗教和象征价值,同时还蕴含着丰富的建筑、考古和艺术意义。

B　①吴哥古迹内部仍有人居住,很多村庄散落其中,其中一些村民的祖先可以追溯到吴哥时期。②吴哥建筑群落囊括了高棉时期所有主要的建筑房屋与水文工程系统,大多数的人工湖和运河在今天依旧存在。③所有的一切都展现了该地遗址的完整性,这一完整性很好地反映了历代城池的辉煌。④然而,遗址的完整性目前正遭受着双重压力:一是超过10万人的居民所形成的内在压力,这些居民散落分布在园区内超过112个历史聚居点,他们不断尝试去扩大自身地盘;二是与暹粒接近带来的外在压力,而暹粒是省会和旅游枢纽。

C ①Angkor is one of the largest archaeological sites in operation in the world. ②Tourism represents an enormous economic potential but it can also generate irreparable destructions of the tangible as well as intangible cultural heritage. ③Many research projects have been undertaken, since the international safeguarding program was first launched in 1993. ④**The scientific objectives of the research (e.g., anthro-pological studies on socio-economic conditions) result in a better knowledge and understanding of the history of the site, and its inhabitants that constitute a rich exceptional legacy of the intangible heritage.** ⑤**The purpose is to associate the "intangible culture" to the enhancement of the monuments in order to sensitize the local population to the importance and necessity of its protection and preservation and assist in the development of the site as Angkor is a living heritage site where Khmer people in general, but especially the local population, are known to be particularly conservative with respect to ancestral traditions and where they adhere to a great number of archaic cultural practices that have disappeared elsewhere.** ⑥Moreover, the Angkor Archaeological Park is very rich in medicinal plants used by the local population for treatment of diseases. ⑦ The plants are prepared and then brought to different temple sites for blessing by the gods. The Preah Khan temple is considered to have been a university of medicine and the Neak Poan an ancient hospital.

C ①吴哥是世界上正在运行的最大的考古遗址之一。②虽然旅游业代表着一种巨大的经济潜力，但它也可能造成无法弥补的对物质文化遗产和非物质文化遗产的毁损。③自1993年国际文化遗产保护计划首次出台以来，许多研究项目纷纷开展。④研究的科学目标（例如对社会经济情况的人类学研究）促进了人们对遗址历史的了解，也增加了人们对当地居民的认识，这些居民构成了这一丰富的非物质遗产的特殊部分。⑤吴哥堪称历史文化的活化石；一般来说，高棉人（特别是当地居民）在保留先辈传统和遵循大量古老文化习俗方面做得非常出色（其中很多习俗在其他地方早已消亡）。因此，开展这些研究旨在将"非物质文化"与历史遗迹的保护联系起来，从而使当地居民意识到吴哥遗迹保护的重要性和必要性，并协助当地遗址的开发工作。⑥此外，吴哥考古公园（Angkor Archaeological Park）内有着种类丰富的药用植物，当地居民用它们治疗疾病。当地居民准备好这些植物后，将其带到不同的寺庙祈求神灵庇佑。⑦圣剑寺（Preah Khan）一向被视为一所医药大学，而尼克潘（Neak Poan）则被认为是一家古老的医院。

重点句子分析

1. With impressive monuments, several different ancient urban plans and large water reservoirs, the site is a unique concentration of features testifying to an

exceptional civilization.

> 第一步　主从分析

主干：the site is a concentration。

修饰：原因状语 with impressive monuments，several different ancient urban plans and large water reservoirs；定语 unique、of features、testifying to an exceptional civilization。

> 第二步　句型解析

A. 状语的处理：原因状语过长，单独处理，确定主语为吴哥。译为"吴哥拥有着令人惊叹的历史遗迹、几处古城池以及大型水库遗址"。

B. 第三处定语的处理：定语较短，前置处理。译为"拥有杰出文明的"。

> 第三步　翻译

吴哥拥有着令人惊叹的历史遗迹、几处古城池以及大型水库遗址，是一个拥有杰出文明且独一无二的特点集中地。

2. The architecture and layout of the successive capitals bear witness to a high level of social order and ranking within the Khmer Empire.

> 第一步　主从分析

主干：the architecture and layout bear witness to social order and ranking。

修饰：定语 of the successive capitals、a high level of、within the Khmer Empire。

> 第二步　句型解析

A. 偏正互换：a high level of social order and ranking 偏正互换，译为"高水平的社会地位和秩序"。

B. 省略：bear 处理为弱动词，省去不译。

C. 词性转换：名词 witness 转换成动词，译为"见证"。

> 第三步　翻译

吴哥延绵的建筑与布局见证了高棉帝国高水平的社会地位和秩序。

3. The park is inhabited, and many villages, in some of whom the ancestors are dating back to the Angkor period, are scattered throughout the park.

> 第一步　主从分析

主句：the park is inhabited，and many villages are scattered。

修饰：定语 in some of whom the ancestors are dating back to the Angkor period；地点状语 throughout the park。

> 第二步　句型解析

A. 被动的处理：采用被动变主动，将 is inhabited 译为"有人居住"；采用有被不用被，将 are scattered 译为"散落在……"。

B. 语序调整：将两个并列的主干部分前置译出。非限制性定语从句过长，后置单独处理

125

作补充说明,译为"其中一些村民的祖先可以追溯到吴哥时期"。

第三步　翻译

吴哥古迹内部仍有人居住,很多村庄散落其中,其中一些村民的祖先可以追溯到吴哥时期。

4. The site integrity however, is put under dual pressures: endogenous, exerted by more than 100,000 inhabitants distributed over 112 historic settlements scattered over the site, who constantly try to expand their dwelling areas; exogenous, related to the proximity of the town of Siem Reap, the seat of the province and a tourism hub.

第一步　主从分析

主干:the site integrity is put under dual pressures: endogenous; exogenous。

修饰:连接性状语 however;定语 exerted by more than 100,000 inhabitants distributed over 112 historic settlements scattered over the site、who constantly try to expand their dwelling areas、related to the proximity of the town of Siem Rea;同位语 the seat of the province and a tourism hub。

第二步　句型解析

A. 同位语的处理:处理为顶针结构;为体现"吴哥"与"暹粒"的差距,增加连接词"而"。译为"而暹粒是省会和旅游枢纽"。

B. 定状互换:定语 scattered 转化成副词状语"散落地"。

C. 词性转换:将名词 proximity 转换为其动词用法"接近"。

D. 第一处定语的处理:循环定语,分别处理。exerted by more than 100,000 inhabitants 前置,译为"超过10万人的居民所形成的";distributed over 112 historic settlements scattered over the site 后置单独处理,译为"这些居民散落分布在园区内超过112个历史聚居点"。

E. 第二处定语的处理:定语从句过长,单独处理,确定主语为"这些居民"。译为"他们不断尝试去扩大自身地盘"。

第三步　翻译

然而,遗址的完整性目前正遭受着双重压力:一是超过10万人的居民所形成的内在压力,这些居民散落分布在园区内超过112个历史聚居点,他们不断尝试去扩大自身地盘;二是与暹粒接近带来的外在压力,而暹粒是省会和旅游枢纽。

5. The scientific objectives of the research (e.g., anthro-pological studies on socio-economic conditions) result in a better knowledge and understanding of the history of the site, and its inhabitants that constitute a rich exceptional legacy of the intangible heritage.

第一步　主从分析

主句：the scientific objectives of the research result in a better knowledge and understanding。

修饰：定语 of the history of the site，and its inhabitants；that constitute a rich exceptional legacy of the intangible heritage；插入语 anthro-pological studies on socio-economic conditions。

第二步　句型解析

A. 词性转换：result in 处理为弱动词，省去不译；形容词 better 转换为动词，根据动宾搭配译为"促进（了解）""增加（认识）"。

B. 增词：增加主语"人们"。

C. 定语的处理：单独成句，确定主语为"这些居民"，译为"这些居民构成了丰富的非物质遗产的特殊部分"。

第三步　翻译

研究的科学目标（例如对社会经济情况的人类学研究）促进了人们对遗址历史的了解，也增加了人们对当地居民的认识，这些居民构成了丰富的非物质遗产的特殊部分。

6. The purpose is to associate the "intangible culture" to the enhancement of the monuments in order to sensitize the local population to the importance and necessity of its protection and preservation and assist in the development of the site as Angkor is a living heritage site where Khmer people in general, but especially the local population, are known to be particularly conservative with respect to ancestral traditions and where they adhere to a great number of archaic cultural practices that have disappeared elsewhere.

第一步　主从分析

主句：the purpose is to associate the "intangible culture" to the enhancement of the monuments。

修饰：目的状语 in order to sensitize the local population to the importance and necessity of its protection and preservation、assist in the development of the site；原因状语从句 as Angkor is a living heritage site where Khmer people in general，but especially the local population，are known to be particularly conservative with respect to ancestral traditions and where they adhere to a great number of archaic cultural practices that have disappeared elsewhere；定语 where Khmer people in general，but especially the local population，are known to be particularly conservative with respect to ancestral traditions、where they adhere to a great number of archaic cultural practices that have disappeared elsewhere、that have disappeared elsewhere；插入语 but especially the local population。

第二步　句型解析

A. 语序调整：长句拆分，结构重塑。将原因状语从句提至句首单独成句，直接增加连接词"因此"使上下文语义贯通。

B. 原因状语从句的处理：主句 Angkor is a living heritage site 单独成句。and 连接的两个定语从句中心词均为 a living heritage site，可合并翻译，单独成句，第三处定语处理为插入语。分别译为"吴哥堪称历史文化的活化石""一般来说，高棉人（特别是当地居民）在保留先辈传统和遵循大量古老文化习俗方面做得非常出色（其中很多习俗在其他地方早已消亡）"。

C. 词性转换：主语 the purpose 动词化为"旨在"，同时增加主语"开展这些研究"。

D. 被动的处理：are known to 被动变主动，译为"做得出色"。

E. 省略：the importance and necessity of its protection and preservation 中的 protection 和 preservation 均为"保护"的意思，无需重复翻译。

第三步　翻译

吴哥堪称历史文化的活化石；一般来说，高棉人（特别是当地居民）在保留先辈传统和遵循大量古老文化习俗方面做得非常出色（其中很多习俗在其他地方早已消亡）。因此，开展这些研究旨在将"非物质文化"与历史遗迹的保护联系起来，从而使当地居民意识到吴哥遗迹保护的重要性和必要性，并协助当地遗址的开发工作。

31.2　Chinese-English Translation

31.2.1　Passage 1

A　①到2020年，老龄事业发展整体水平明显提升，养老体系更加健全完善，及时应对、科学应对、综合应对人口老龄化的社会基础更加牢固。②老龄事业发展和养老体系建设的法治化、信息化、标准化、规范化程度明显提高。③市场活力和社会创造力得到充分激发，养老服务和产品供给主体更加多元、内容更加丰富、质量更加优良，以信用为核心的新型市场监管机制建立完善。

A　①By the year of 2020, the overall development of the career of elderly care will see prominent improvement. A more sophisticated system will be fostered along with the sounder social foundations for tackling the aging problem in a way that is timely, practical and comprehensive. ②The overall development of the elder career and the institutional construction of the corresponding system will see major progress in terms of legalization, informatization, standardization and normalization. ③Market vitality and social creativity will be fully energized for more diversified providers of elderly care services and products and more abundant and quality offerings, with a new type of market regulation institution with honesty at its core being in place.

B ①全社会积极应对人口老龄化、自觉支持老龄事业发展和养老体系建设的意识、意愿显著增强,敬老、养老助老社会风尚更加浓厚,安全绿色、便利、舒适的老年宜居环境建设扎实推进,老年文化体育教育事业更加繁荣发展,老年人合法权益得到有效保护,老年人参与社会发展的条件持续改善。

B ①The whole society will be more active in coping with the aging problem with stronger awareness and willingness to support the development of elderly care and its institutional construction. The social moral atmosphere of respecting, caring and helping senior citizens will be better fostered. Steady progress will be made in constructing a safe, green, convenient and comfortable environment for the senior citizens to live in, so as to safeguard the prosperity of elderly culture, P. E. and education and effectively protect senior citizens' legitimate rights and interests, gradually optimizing the conditions for senior citizens to participate in social development.

重点句子分析

1. 到 2020 年,老龄事业发展整体水平明显提升,养老体系更加健全完善,及时应对、科学应对、综合应对人口老龄化的社会基础更加牢固。

第一步 主从分析

主干:发展水平提升,体系健全完善。

修饰:时间状语"到 2020 年";定语"老龄事业""整体""养老";评注性状语"明显""更加";结果状语"及时应对、科学应对、综合应对人口老龄化的社会基础更加牢固"。

第二步 句型解析

A. 确定关键动词:"提升"采用 see ... improvement 结构;"健全完善"采用被动语态,译为 be fostered。

B. 省略范畴词:"水平"属于范畴词,英译时可以省略。

C. 定状互换:副词状语"及时、科学、综合"转换为定语,译为 in a way that is timely, practical and comprehensive。

第三步 翻译

By the year of 2020, the overall development of the career of elderly care will see prominent improvement. A more sophisticated system will be fostered along with the sounder social foundations for tackling the aging problem in a way that is timely, practical and comprehensive.

2. 市场活力和社会创造力得到充分激发,养老服务和产品供给主体更加多元、内容更加丰富、质量更加优良,以信用为核心的新型市场监管机制建立完善。

第一步　主从分析

主干:活力和创造力得到激发。

修饰:定语"市场""社会""以信用为核心的新型""养老服务和产品";评注性状语"充分""更加";目的状语"养老服务和产品供给主体更加多元、内容更加丰富、质量更加优良";结果状语"以信用为核心的新型市场监管机制建立完善"。

第二步　句型解析

A. 定语的处理:"以信用为核心的新型"后置处理,译为 with honesty at its core。

B. 主动变被动:中文多主动,英文多被动。"得到激发"转换为被动语态,译为 be energized。

C. 结果状语的处理:处理为非谓语形式,译为 bringing more abundant and quality offerings。

第三步　翻译

Market vitality and social creativity will be fully energized for more diversified providers of elderly care services and products and more abundant and quality offerings, with a new type of market regulation institution with honesty at its core being in place.

3. 安全绿色、便利、舒适的老年宜居环境建设扎实推进,老年文化体育教育事业更加繁荣发展,老年人合法权益得到有效保护,老年人参与社会发展的条件持续改善。

第一步　主从分析

主干:进步将被实现。

修饰:定语"扎实";方式状语"安全绿色、便利、舒适的老年宜居环境建设";目的状语"老年文化体育教育事业更加繁荣发展,老年人合法权益得到有效保护";结果状语"老年人参与社会发展的条件持续改善。"

第二步　句型解析

A. 词性转换:将名词"建设"转化为动词 construct;副词"繁荣"转化为名词 prosperity;动词"发展"转化为名词,定为范畴词,省略不译。

B. 被动的处理:"得到保护"被动变主动,直接译为 protect。

第三步　翻译

Steady progress will be made in constructing a safe, green, convenient and comfortable environment for the senior citizens to live in, so as to safeguard the prosperity of elderly culture, P. E. and education and effectively protect senior citizens' legitimate rights and interests, gradually optimizing the conditions for senior citizens to participate in social development.

31.2.2　Passage 2

A ①中国的改革开放发端于农村,目的是调节农民和土地之间的关系。②1978年之前,数亿中国人还在为温饱问题发愁。经40年的发展,中国有7亿多农村贫困人口脱贫。③从1978年到1985年,中国农村经济体制的深刻变革,为农村经济的增长和贫困人口的大幅减少提供了强劲动力。④按当时的标准,有50%未解决温饱的农村人口在这期间解决了温饱问题。⑤按现在的扶贫标准,有超过1亿农村人口在这期间摆脱了贫困。⑥这不仅为全面建成小康社会打下了坚实的基础,而且为全人类的扶贫和发展做出了巨大贡献。

B ①1978年,安徽凤阳县小岗村的18户农民走出了中国农村改革的第一步,破除了计划经济体制的诸多束缚,实行以家庭联产承包责任制为基础的家庭经营,获得了可以自由耕种的承包土地,极大地调动了生产积极性,使他们以巨大的热情投入到农业生产之中。

A ①China's reform originated from the rural areas, aiming to coordinate the relationship between the rural demography and land. ②Before the year of 1978, hundreds of millions of Chinese people still struggled to meet the subsistence level. Nowadays, after over forty years' development, more than seven hundred million rural populations have been lifted out of poverty in China. ③From 1978 to 1985, the rural economic system had undergone profound changes in China, providing robust impetus for rural economic development and significant poverty reduction. ④By the standard at that time, 50 percent of the rural population who were under the subsistence level successfully transcended that poverty line. ⑤By the poverty reduction standard now, more than one hundred million rural people got rid of poverty during that period. ⑥This not only laid a solid foundation for China to build a moderately prosperous society in all respects, but also made great contributions to poverty alleviation and development for all mankind.

B ①In the year of 1978, 18 rural households in the Xiaogang Village, Fengyang County, Anhui Province took the first step of China's rural reform to breakdown various restraints posed by the planned economy. They started household-based operation with the household contract responsibility system as its basis and gained contracted land that allowed free cultivation, greatly enhancing peasants morale and enthusiasm in agricultural production.

重点句子分析

1. 从1978年到1985年,中国农村经济体制的深刻变革,为农村经济的增长和贫困人口的大幅减少提供了强劲动力。

<u>第一步　主从分析</u>

主干:经济体制变革。

修饰:时间状语"从1978年到1985年";定语"农村""深刻""强劲";结果状语"为农村经济的增长和贫困人口的大幅减少提供了强劲动力";地点状语"中国"。

<u>第二步　句型解析</u>

A. 确定关键动词:"变革"译为undergo changes,"提供"译为provide。

B. 结果状语的处理:处理为非谓语形式,译为providing robust impetus for rural economic development and significant poverty reduction。

<u>第三步　翻译</u>

From 1978 to 1985, the rural economic system had undergone profound changes in China, providing robust impetus for rural economic development and significant poverty reduction.

2. 按当时的标准,有50%未解决温饱的农村人口在这期间解决了温饱问题。

<u>第一步　主从分析</u>

主干:人口解决了温饱问题。

修饰:方式状语"按当时的标准";定语"有50%""未解决温饱的""农村";时间状语"在这期间"。

<u>第二步　句型解析</u>

A. 定语的处理:"未解决温饱的"后置处理为定语从句,译为who were under the subsistence level。

B. 文化负载词的处理:"解决了温饱问题"意译为transcended that poverty line。

<u>第三步　翻译</u>

By the standard at that time, 50 percent of the rural population who were under the subsistence level successfully transcended that poverty line.

3. 1978年,安徽凤阳县小岗村的18户农民走出了中国农村改革的第一步,破除了计划经济体制的诸多束缚,实行以家庭联产承包责任制为基础的家庭经营,获得了可以自由耕种的承包土地,极大地调动了生产积极性,使他们以巨大的热情投入到农业生产之中。

第一步　主从分析

主干:农民走出了第一步;农民实行了家庭经营、获得了承包土地。

修饰:时间状语"1978 年";结果状语"破除了计划经济体制的诸多束缚""极大地调动了生产积极性,使他们以巨大的热情投入到农业生产之中";定语"安徽凤阳县小岗村的""18 户""中国农村改革的""计划经济体制的""以家庭联产承包责任制为基础的""可以自由耕种的"。

第二步　句型解析

A. 断句:本句较长,根据句意可划分为"1978 年,安徽凤阳县小岗村的 18 户农民走出了中国农村改革的第一步,破除了计划经济体制的诸多束缚。"和"农民实行以家庭联产承包责任制为基础的家庭经营,获得了可以自由耕种的承包土地,极大地调动了生产积极性,使他们以巨大的热情投入到农业生产之中。"两个单独的句子。

B. 定语的处理:定语"18 户"较短,前置处理;定语"安徽凤阳县小岗村的""中国农村改革的""计划经济体制的""以家庭联产承包责任制为基础的""可以自由耕种的"较长,均后置处理,分别译为 in the Xiaogang Village, Fengyang County, Anhui Province、of China's rural reform、posed by the planned economy、with the household contract responsibility system as its basis、that allowed free cultivation。

C. 结果状语的处理:结果状语一处理为不定式结构,译为 to breakdown various restraints posed by the planned economy;结果状语另一处理为非谓语结构,译为 greatly enhancing peasants morale and enthusiasm in agricultural production。

D. 定状互换:地点状语"到农业生产中"转换为定语,译为 in agricultural production。

第三步　翻译

In the year of 1978, 18 rural households in the Xiaogang Village, Fengyang County, Anhui Province took the first step of China's rural reform to breakdown various restraints posed by the planned economy. They started household-based operation with the household contract responsibility system as its basis and gained contracted land that allowed free cultivation, greatly enhancing peasants morale and enthusiasm in agricultural production.

32 2021年11月二级笔译真题

32.1 English-Chinese Translation

32.1.1 Passage 1

A ①A spectre haunts this book—the spectre of Europe. ②**Just as the 700 pages of Tony Blair's autobiography could not escape the shadow of Iraq, so the 700 pages of David Cameron's memoir are destined to be read through a single lens: Brexit.**

B ①**For all its detailed accounts of coalition talks with the leader of the liberal Democrats or Syria debates with Barack Obama, Brexit is the story.** ②Cameron acknowledges as much, writing several times that he goes over the events that led to the leave vote of 2016 everyday, "over and over again. Reliving and rethinking the decisions, rerunning alternatives and what-might-have-beens." ③Later he writes: "My regrets about what had happened went deep. I knew then that they would never leave. And they never have."

C ①**It's this which gives the book its narrative arc, one it shares with Blairs.** ②Both tell the story of a man whose previously charmed path to success is suddenly interrupted, running into a catastrophe that will haunt him to his last breath. ③The development is the same in both cases, a series of consecutive victories-winning his party's leadership, rebranding and modernizing that party to appeal to the center

A ①这本自传有个摆脱不掉的幽灵—欧洲问题。②正如托尼·布莱尔(Tony Blair)700页的自传无法摆脱伊拉克问题的阴影一样,大卫·卡梅伦(David Cameron)那长达700页的自传也注定会从脱欧这个单一角度进行解读。

B ①尽管这本自传详细地讲述了卡梅伦和自由民主党领袖组建联合政府的谈判,以及卡梅伦与奥巴马有关叙利亚问题的辩论,但是以上这些都是围绕脱欧进行论述的。②卡梅伦也承认了这一点,好几处都写到自己每天都在反复回顾引发2016年脱欧公投的一系列事件,"我一遍又一遍回忆,重温并反思当时做的决定,重新推演其他替代方案以及这些方案可能导致的结果。"③后来他写道:"对于已经发生的事情,我深表遗憾。那时我就知道后悔将会伴随我终生。直到现在,后悔从未离开我。"

C ①正是脱欧这件事给予了这本书叙事弧,这种叙事弧与布莱尔的自传不谋而合。②这两本自传都讲述了一个男人的故事,主角径情直遂、成就辉煌,倏忽间成功戛然而止,闯下弥天大祸,势穷力竭最终抱憾终身。③这两本书

134

ground, reaching Downing Street, winning re-election—only to make a decision that will wreak lasting havoc.

D ①Cameron offers the same defence for Brexit that Blair gave for Iraq: yes, thing might have turned out disastrously, but my mistake was honest, I acted in good faith, I only did what I truly believed was right.

E ①Which is not to say that the memoir is not self-critical. ②On the contrary, Cameron scolds himself throughout and not only on Brexit. ③He writes that he often misses the wood for the trees, getting lost in policy detail and failing "to see the bigger, emotional picture".

F ①Nevertheless, his memoir reminds you why Cameron dominated British politics for so long. ②The prose is, like him, smooth and efficient. ③The Chapter describing the short life and death of the Cameron's severely disabled son, Ivan, is almost unbearably moving. ④**With admirable honesty, Cameron admits that the period of mourning did not only follows his son's death but his birth,** "trying to come to terms with the difference between the child you expected and longed for and the reality that you now face". ⑤What, had, until then, been a charmed life was interrupted by the deep heartbreak.

有一样的情节发展,先是取得一连串的胜利——当选一党之首,重塑政党形象,完成政党现代化改造以吸引中立选民,入主唐宁街首相府邸,再是成功连任——最后却做了一个后患无穷的决定。

D ①卡梅伦为英国脱欧所做的辩解,和布莱尔在伊拉克问题上的辩解如出一辙:是的,事情可能会变得糟糕,但这只是无心之失,我做事诚恳,只是做了我认为正确的事。

E ①这并不是说卡梅伦的自传没有自我批评。②相反,卡梅伦自始至终都在责怪自己,而且不仅仅局限于脱欧问题。③他在自传中写道,自己一叶障目,不见森林,迷失在政策的细节中,却未能统筹全局,把控情绪。

F ①尽管如此,卡梅伦的自传依然提醒了读者他能在英国长期执政的原因。②卡梅伦自传行文紧凑流畅,文如其人。③书中有一章讲述了卡梅伦严重残疾的儿子伊万短暂的一生及其离世,令人动容。④带着令人敬佩的坦诚,卡梅伦承认哀恸之情不仅仅是从自己儿子去世时开始,也是从他出生时开始。"我试图接受这种差异,你所期待和渴望的孩子与面临的现实的差异。"⑤卡梅伦此前风光无限的人生到此戛然而止。

重点句子分析

1. **Just as the 700 pages of Tony Blair's autobiography could not escape the shadow of Iraq, so the 700 pages of David Cameron's memoir are destined to be read through a single lens: Brexit.**

第一步　主从分析

主干：the 700 pages of David Cameron's memoir are destined to be read。

修饰：比较状语从句 just as the 700 pages of Tony Blair's autobiography could not escape the shadow of Iraq；方式状语 through a single lens；同位语 Brexit。

第二步　句型解析

A. 增加范畴词：the shadow of Iraq 原本指"伊拉克的阴影"，此处增加一个范畴词，变成"伊拉克问题的阴影"，使译文更加流畅。

B. 词意选择：lens 原本是透镜、镜片的意思，根据句中语境处理为"角度"。

C. 被动的处理：可以采用"有被不用被"的形式，将 to be read 译为"进行解读"。

第三步　翻译

正如托尼·布莱尔（Tony Blair）700 页的自传无法摆脱伊拉克问题的阴影一样，大卫·卡梅伦（David Cameron）那长达 700 页的自传也注定会从脱欧这个单一角度进行解读。

2. For all its detailed accounts of coalition talks with the leader of the liberal Democrats or Syria debates with Barack Obama, Brexit is the story.

第一步　主从分析

主干：Brexit is the story。

修饰：让步状语 for all its detailed accounts of coalition talks with the leader of the liberal Democrats or Syria debates with Barack Obama。

第二步　句型解析

A. 代词的处理：its 指代上文中的 the 700 pages of David Cameron's memoir，译为"这本自传"。

B. 词性转换：accounts 原本是名词，英译汉处理成动词；detailed 原本是形容词用来修饰 accounts，英到中转变成副词，完整翻译为"详细地讲述了"。

C. 逻辑关系：让步状语和主句间存在着转折关系，在译文中通过"尽管"和"但是"两词体现出来。

D. 专有名词的处理：coalition talks 是指 2010 年 5 月英国举行大选，保守党为了上台执政转而同自由民主党谋求谈判组建联合政府，因此在翻译中处理为"和自由民主党领袖组建联合政府的谈判"。

第三步　翻译

尽管这本自传详细地讲述了卡梅伦和自由民主党领袖组建联合政府的谈判，以及卡梅伦与奥巴马总统有关叙利亚问题的辩论，但是以上这些都是围绕脱欧进行论述的。

3. It's this which gives the book its narrative arc, one it shares with Blairs.

第一步　主从分析

主干：it's this which... 。

修饰：同位语 one；定语 which gives the book its narrative arc（修饰 this）、it shares with Blairs（修饰 one）。

第二步　句型解析

A. 代词的处理：this 指代"脱欧"。

B. 同位语的处理：原文中 one 作 narrative 的同位语，在翻译时采用顶针的方法。

第三步　翻译

正是脱欧这件事给予了这本书叙事弧，这种叙事弧和布莱尔的自传中的一样。

4. With admirablehonesty, Cameron admits that the period of mourning did not only follows his son's death but his birth, "trying to come to terms with the difference between the child you expected and longed for and the reality that you now face".

第一步　主从分析

主干：Cameron admits that…。

宾语从句主干：the period of mourning did not only follows his son's death but his birth。

修饰：评注性状语 with admirable honesty；插入语 trying to come to terms with the difference between the child you expected and longed for and the reality that you now face；定语 you expected（修饰 the child）、that you now face（修饰 the reality）。

第二步　句型解析

A. come to terms 的处理：译为"妥协、让步"。

B. 插入语的处理：插入语过长，翻译时可单独成句。

第三步　翻译

带着令人敬佩得坦诚，卡梅伦承认哀恸之情不仅仅是从自己儿子去世时开始，也是从他出生时开始。"我试图接受这种差异，你所期待和渴望的孩子与面临的现实的差异。"

5. What, had, until then, been a charmed life was interrupted by the deep heartbreak.

第一步　主从分析

主干：what had been a life was interrupted。

修饰：时间状语 until then；定语 charmed，修饰 life；方式状语 by the deep heartbreak，修饰 was interrupted。

第二步　句型解析

A. 时间状语的处理：until then 提到句首，翻译为"直到那时"。

B. 时态的处理：原文中使用了过去完成时，在译文中用"此前"两字来体现时态。

C. 被动语态的处理：直接处理，将 was interrupted 翻译为"被打断"，因为中文中被动语态含有贬义色彩,契合原文语境,因此直接处理即可。

第三步　翻译

直到那时,此前其拥有的非常辉煌的人生被深切的悲痛所打断。

32.1.2　Passage 2

A　①A new United Nations Environment Programme（UNEP）report, jointly produced with the International Resources Panel（国际资源小组）, says that a type of unbridled international trade is having a damaging effect not only on rainforests but the entire planet. ②**The report, which called for a raft of new Earth-friendly trade rules, found that the extraction of natural resources could spark water shortages, drive animals to extinction and accelerate climate change—all of which would be ruinous to the global economy.**

B　①**The economic fallout of COVID-19 is just an overture to what we would see if the Earth's natural systems break down.** ②We have to make sure that our global trade policies protect the environment not only for the sake of our planet but also for the long-term health of our economies.

C　①With the demand for natural resources set to double by 2060, the report called on policy makers to embrace what is known as a "circular" economic model. ②That would see business use fewer resources, recycle more and extend the life of their products. ③It would also put an onus on consumers to buy less, save energy and repair things that are broken instead of throwing them directly.

D　①**While the circular model could have "economic implications" for countries that depend on natural resources, it would give rise to new industries devoted to recycling and repairing.** ②Overall, the report predicts a greener economic model would boost

A　①一份由联合国环境规划署与国际资源委员会联合制作的新报告称,不受约束的国际贸易方式不仅对雨林,而且对整个地球都产生着破坏性影响。②这份报告呼吁制定一套新的地球友好型贸易规则,因为它发现开采自然资源可能引发水资源短缺、促使动物灭绝和加速气候变化等问题,这一切对于全球经济而言都有可能是毁灭性的。

B　①新冠肺炎疫情的经济影响只是序曲,如果地球自然系统崩溃,我们将看到的不止于此。②我们必须确保全球贸易政策能够保护环境,不仅为了保护地球,也是为了维持经济的长期健康发展。

C　①鉴于人类对自然资源的需求至2060年将翻一番,该报告呼吁政策制定者们采纳人们所熟知的"循环"经济模式。②这一经济模式将确保企业减少资源利用,加大资源的循环力度,并延长产品的使用寿命。③这同样给消费者们一种责任——减少购买、节约能源、修补破损物品而不是把它们直接扔掉。

D　①虽然循环模式可能会给依赖自然资源的国家带来"经济影响",但同时它也会催生新型回收产业和维修产业。②总的来说,该报告预测,到2060年,这种更为

growth by 8 percent by 2060. ③There's this idea out there, that we have to log, mine, and drill our way to prosperity. ④But that's not true. ⑤By embracing circular economy and reusing material, we can still drive economic growth while protecting the planet for future generations.

E ①Some countries, both in the developed and developing world, have embraced the concept of a circular economy. ②But the report said international trade agreements can play an important role in making those systems more common. ③It called on the World Trade Organization, which has 164 member countries, to take the environment into consideration when setting regulations. ④It also recommends that regional trade pacts promote investment in planet-friendly industries, eliminate "harmful" subsidies, like those for fossil fuels, and avoid undercutting global environmental accords.

F ①Re-orienting the global environment isn't an easy job. ②There are a lot of vested interest we have to contend with. ③But with the Earth's population expected to reach almost 10 billion by 2050, we need to find ways to relieve the pressure on the planet.

绿色环保的经济模型将会给全球带来8%的经济增长。③外界有这么一种看法,即要想经济繁荣,就必须砍伐树木、挖采矿石、钻探石油。④但事实并非如此。⑤通过推行循环经济,重复利用材料,我们在为后代保护地球的同时,仍然可以实现经济增长。

E ①有些发达国家和发展中国家已经接受了循环经济的理念。②但是该报告指出,国际贸易协议可以在推广这些体系时发挥重要作用。③报告呼吁拥有164个成员国的世界贸易组织在制定贸易规则时要考虑到环境因素。④它还建议区域贸易协定应鼓励对地球友好型产业的投资,摒弃诸如对化石燃料的"有害"补贴,并避免破坏世界环境公约。

F ①重新谋划全球环境发展方向并非易事。②还有许多我们必须应对的与既得利益集团之间的博弈。③但随着地球人口预计在2050年之前接近100亿,我们需要找到能缓解地球压力的途径。

重点句子分析

1. The report, which called for a raft of new Earth-friendly trade rules, found that the extraction of natural resources could spark water shortages, drive animals to extinction and accelerate climate change—all of which would be ruinous to the global economy.

第一步　主从分析

主干:the report found that… 。

宾语从句主干:the extraction of natural resources could spark water shortages, drive animals to extinction and accelerate climate change。

修饰:定语 which called for a raft of new Earth-friendly trade rules,修饰 the report;解释性状语 all of which would be ruinous to the global economy。

第二步　句型解析

A. 主语部分的定语从句过长,与主语联系单独成句。

B. extraction 的处理:处理为动词"开放"。

C. 增加动词:of 短语前增加动词"制定"。

D. 增加范畴词:"水资源短缺、促使动物灭绝和加速气候变化"后增加"等问题"。

E. 逻辑关系:因果关系。

第三步　翻译

这份报告呼吁制定一套新的地球友好型贸易规则,因为它发现开采自然资源可能引发水资源短缺、促使动物灭绝和加速气候变化等问题,这一切对于全球经济而言都有可能是毁灭性的。

2. The economic fallout of COVID-19 is just an overture to what we would see if the Earth's natural systems break down.

第一步　主从分析

主干:the fallout is just an overture。

修饰:定语 economic(修饰 fallout)、of COVID-19(修饰 fallout)、to what we would see if the Earth's natural systems break down(修饰 an overture)。

第二步　句型解析

A. 定语的处理:先翻译介词短语后置定语 of COVID-19,再翻译前置定语 economic,即译为"新冠肺炎疫情的经济影响"。

B. 第三处定语中条件状语从句的处理:前置,译为"如果地球自然系统崩溃"。

C. 增词:联系句意增添"不止于此"以使句子完整。

第三步　翻译

新冠肺炎疫情的经济影响只是序曲,如果地球自然系统崩溃,我们将看到的不止于此。

3. While the circular model could have "economic implications" for countries that depend on natural resources, it would give rise to new industries devoted to recycling and repairing.

第一步　主从分析

主干:it would give rise to new industries。

修饰:让步状语 While the circular model could have 'economic implications' for countries that depend on natural resources;定语 that depend on natural resources(修饰 countries)、 devoted to recycling and repairing(修饰 industries)。

第二步　句型解析

A. 第一处定语的处理：前置译为"依赖自然资源的"。

B. 第二处定语的处理：前置译为"致力于回收和修护的"。

C. 逻辑关系：转折关系。

第三步　翻译

虽然循环模式可能会给依赖自然资源的国家带来"经济影响"，但它会催生新的致力于回收和修护的产业。

32.2　Chinese-English Translation

32.2.1　Passage　1

A　①据北京市妇女联合会（Beijing Women's Federation）是北京地区各族各界妇女的群众组织，也是中华全国妇女联合会的地方组织。②其基本职能是代表和维护妇女权益，促进男女平等。③北京市妇联的最高权力机构是北京市妇女代表大会，每五年举行一次。④北京市第十四次妇女代表大会于2019年6月18日开幕。

B　①过去五年，北京市认真贯彻男女平等的基本国策，制定了一系列惠及妇女儿童的法规政策，大力实施妇女儿童发展规划，持续完善妇女工作的科学机制，领导和支持妇联改革不断取得新成效。②当前，北京正努力把北京市建成国际一流的和谐宜居之都。③要实现这个目标，需要包括妇女在内的全市人民共同奋斗。

A　①Beijing Women's Federation is a civil society organization that champions the advancement of women across all sectors in Beijing, and a local branch of the All-China Women's Federation. ②Its basic functions are to represent and protect the rights and interests of women, and promote gender equality. ③The Beijing Women's Congress, held every five years, is the highest authority of BWF, ④and the 14th session kicked off on June 18, 2019.

B　①In line with the basic national policy of gender equality, Beijing over the past five years has introduced a series of legislations and regulations for the benefit of women and children, vigorously implemented plans for their development, and continuously improved mechanisms for promoting women's work. As a result, it has scored impressive gains in the reform of BWF. ②Currently, Beijing is striving to build itself into a world-class, harmonious and habitable capital. ③Realization of this goal requires the joint efforts of all residents in the whole city, including women.

C　①Women's federations at all levels in Beijing should earnestly study and implement Xi Jinping's important remarks on women and women's work, thus further enhancing their sense of responsibility and mission. In addition, they need to serve the overall interests and deepen their reforms in order to

C ①北京市各级妇联组织应认真学习贯彻习近平总书记关于妇女和妇女工作的重要论述,进一步增强责任感和使命感,坚持服务大局,深化妇联改革,充分发挥妇女的"两个独特作用",维护妇女合法权益,帮助她们解决最关心最直接最现实的利益问题。②同时鼓励广大妇女践行社会主义核心价值观,坚守社会公德、职业道德,弘扬家庭美德、个人品德,传承中华民族传统美德,积极引领文明风尚,鼓励妇女踏实干事创业,做自信自立自强的新时代女性。

give full play to women's role in social and family life, safeguard the rights and interests of women, and solve the problems that concern women the most. ②At the same time, federations at all levels should encourage women to practice the socialist core values, stick to social morality and professional ethics, carry forward family virtues and personal characters, inherit the traditional virtues of the Chinese nation, and actively lead the civilized style. The federations should also motivate them to work or start their own businesses in a down-to-earth manner so as to be women with self-independent, self-confidence and self-reliance in the new era.

重点句子分析

1. 过去五年,北京市认真贯彻男女平等的基本国策,制定了一系列惠及妇女儿童的法规政策,大力实施妇女儿童发展规划,持续完善妇女工作的科学机制,领导和支持妇联改革不断取得新成效。

第一步 主从分析

主干:北京市贯彻国策,制定法规政策,实施发展规划,完善科学机制,领导和支持改革取得成效。

修饰:时间状语"过去五年";修饰性状语"认真""大力""持续";定语"男女平等的"(修饰"基本国策")、"一系列惠及妇女儿童的"(修饰"法规政策")、"妇女儿童"(修饰"发展规划")、"妇女工作的"(修饰"科学机制")。

第二步 句型解析

A. 关键动词的确定:"制定"译为 introduce;"完善"译为 improve。

B. 关键副词的确定:"大力"译为 vigorously。

C.逻辑关系:"贯彻男女平等的基本国策,制定了一系列惠及妇女儿童的法规政策,大力实施妇女儿童发展规划,持续完善妇女工作的科学机制"和"领导和支持妇联改革不断取得新成效"构成因果关系。

第三步 翻译

In line with the basic national policy of gender equality, Beijing over the past five years has introduced a series of legislations and regulations for the benefit of women and children, vigorously implemented plans for their development, and continuously improved mechanisms for the advancement of women. As a result, it has achieved new gains in the perspective of leading and supporting the reform of BWF.

2. 北京市各级妇联组织应认真学习贯彻习近平总书记关于妇女和妇女工作的重要论述,进一步增强责任感和使命感,坚持服务大局,深化妇联改革,充分发挥妇女的"两个独特作用",维护妇女合法权益,帮助她们解决最关心最直接最现实的利益问题。

第一步 主从分析

主干:妇联组织学习贯彻习近平总书记论述,坚持服务大局,深化妇联改革。

修饰:结果状语"进一步增强责任感和使命感";目的状语"充分发挥妇女的'两个独特作用',维护妇女合法权益,帮助她们解决最关心最直接最现实的利益问题";定语"北京市各级"(修饰"妇联组织")、"习近平总书记关于妇女和妇女工作的"(修饰"重要论述")、"最关心最直接最现实的"(修饰"利益问题")。

第二步 句型解析

A.断句处理:根据意群划分,将句子划分为两句,第一句在"增强责任感和使命感"结束。

B."两个独特作用"的处理:不能简单翻译为 two special roles,这里的两个指的是家庭和社会,应译为 women's role in social and family life。

C.目的状语的处理:用 in order to 连接。

D.定语的处理:均后置处理。

第三步 翻译

Women's federations at all levels in Beijing should earnestly study and implement Xi Jinping's important remarks on women and women's work, thus further strengthening their sense of responsibility and mission. They should also insist on serving the overall interests and deepen their reforms in order to give full play to women's role in social and family life, safeguard the rights and interests of women, and solve the problems that concern women the most.

32.2.2 Passage 2

A ①"十三五"期间,中国坚定不移走生态优先、绿色发展之路,全力以赴建设人与自然和谐共生的现代化。

B ①第一,建制度,立规章,依靠法治护航绿色发展。②近年来,从生态环境损害赔偿到生态环境保护督察,从修订大气污染防治法到民法典,都充分体现绿色发展理念,并出台了60多项相关配套制度,构建起完善的生态环境法律框架,为绿色发展提供有力支撑。

C ①第二,治污染,调结构,坚决打好污染防治攻坚战。②5年来,我国向污染宣战,实施大气、水、土壤污染防治三大攻坚战。③不断创新污染防治方式,不断拓展防治领域,加大防治力度。④2019年,全国重点城市 $PM_{2.5}$ 和二氧化硫平均浓度分别比2013年下降43%和73%,重污染天数下降81%。⑤蓝天越来越多,水质越来越好,生态环境越来越美。

D ①第三,划红线,筑牢生态屏障,夯实高质量发展的绿色基础。②近年来,各地纷纷发布生态环境管控方案。③如今,25%的陆地国土面积已被划入生态保护红线,并建立了118万处自然保护区,占陆地国土面积的18%。

E ①随着这些政策和措施的落实,经济社会发展和生态环境保护逐步走向双赢。

A ①Over the period of the 13th Five-Year Plan (2016—2020), China has stayed committed to green development with a particular focus on ecological conservation, and devoted itself to achieving modernization marked by the harmonious coexistence between man and nature.

B ①Firstly, we should set up systems and regulations to safeguard green development by the rule of law. ②In recent years, we have taken actions from the enaction of ecological and environmental damage compensation to the inspection on ecological and environmental protection, from the revision of the Law on the Prevention and Control of Atmospheric Pollution to the formulation of the Civil Code; all of them fully embodies the philosophy of green development. Besides, more than 60 supporting institutions have been established to construct a sound framework for ecological conservation laws to support green development.

C ①Secondly, we should fight effectively in the critical battle against pollution through addressing pollution and readjusting industrial structure. ②Over the past five years, China declared a war against pollution and fought effectively in the three critical battles against air, water and soil pollution. ③We have been continuously innovating methods, expanding coverage and intensifying efforts in terms of preventing and addressing pollution. ④In 2019, the average concentrations of $PM_{2.5}$ and sulfur dioxide in key cities of China were 43% and 73% lower than that of 2013 respectively, while the number of days with heavy pollution decreased by 81%. ⑤As a result, there has been a noticeable increase in the number of blue-sky days, while the water quality and the overall eco-environment are ever improving.

D ①Thirdly, we should set the ecological red line as a benchmark in conservation to cement the green foundation of high-quality development. ②Over the past few years, local authorities have issued their ecological management and control plans. ③So far, 25% of the country's land area has been brought under the red line for ecological protection, and 11,800 natural reserves have been built, accounting for 18% of the land area.

E ①With the rollout of these policies and measures, we will achieve win-win results in both economic-social development and ecological protection.

重点句子分析

1. 近年来,从生态环境损害赔偿到生态环境保护督察,从修订大气污染防治法到民法典,都充分体现绿色发展理念,并出台了 60 多项相关配套制度,构建起完善的生态环境法律框架,为绿色发展提供有力支撑。

第一步　主从分析

主干:我们的行动都体现了绿色发展理念;制度出台了。

修饰:时间状语"近年来";方式状语"从生态环境损害赔偿到生态环境保护督察,从修订大气污染防治法到民法典";评注性状语"都充分";定语"60 多项相关配套";结果状语"构建起完善的生态环境法律框架""为绿色发展提供有力支撑"。

第二步　句型解析

A. 断句处理:由于句子太长,将其分成两句来翻译,从"绿色发展理念"处断句。

B. 结果状语的处理:可以处理为不定式的形式。

第三步　翻译

In recent years, we have taken actions from the enaction of ecological and environmental damage compensation to the inspection on ecological and environmental protection, from the revision of the Law on the Prevention and Control of Atmospheric Pollution to the formulation of the Civil Code, all of them fully embodies the philosophy of green development. Besides, more than 60 supporting institutions have been established to construct a sound framework for ecological conservation laws to support green development.

2. 2019 年,全国重点城市 $PM_{2.5}$ 和二氧化硫平均浓度分别比 2013 年下降 43% 和 73%,重污染天数下降 81%。

第一步　主从分析

主干:$PM_{2.5}$ 和二氧化硫平均浓度下降 43% 和 73%,重污染天数下降 81%。

修饰:时间状语"2019 年";地点状语"全国重点城市";比较状语"分别比 2013 年"。

第二步　句型解析

A. 逻辑关系:并列。

B. 名词的选择:浓度译为 concentration。

C. 两个"下降"的处理:前一个下降比较的是"浓度",译为 were...lower;后一个比较的是"天数",译为 decrease。

> 第三步　翻译

In 2019, the average concentrations of PM₂.₅ and sulfur dioxide in key cities of China were 43% and 73% lower than that of 2013 respectively, while the number of days with heavy pollution decreased by 81%.

3. 如今,25%的陆地国土面积已被划入生态保护红线,并建立了118万处自然保护区,占陆地国土面积的18%。

> 第一步　主从分析

主干:25%的陆地国土面积被划入红线,并建立了自然保护区。
修饰:时间状语"如今";定语"生态保护";评注性状语"占陆地国土面积的18%"。

> 第二步　句型解析

A. 评注性状语的处理:译为分词结构。
B. 无主语句"并建立了118万处自然保护区",处理为被动。

> 第三步　翻译

So far, 25% of the country's land area has been brought under the red line for ecological protection, and 11,800 natural reserves have been built, accounting for 18% of the land area.

主要参考文献

陈定安,2004.翻译精要[M].北京:中国青年出版社.
何刚强,1998.现代英汉翻译操作[M].北京:北京大学出版社.
胡壮麟,1994.语篇的衔接与连贯[M].上海:上海外语教育出版社.
毛荣贵,2003.新世纪大学英汉翻译教程[M].上海:上海交通大学出版社.
毛荣贵,2003.英译汉技巧新编[M].北京:外文出版社.
秦荻辉,2001.科技英语写作教程[M].西安:西安电子科技大学出版.
宋天锡,2003.翻译新概念英汉互译实用教程[M].北京:中国国防工业出版社.
孙致礼,2003.新编英汉翻译教程[M].上海:上海外语教育出版社.
倜西,董乐山,张宁,2002.英汉翻译手册[M].北京:商务印书馆.
魏志成,2004.英汉比较翻译教程练习[M].北京:清华大学出版社.
许建平,2000.英汉互译实践与技巧[M].北京:清华大学出版社.
叶子南,2001.高级英汉翻译理论与实践[M].2版.北京:清华大学出版社.
杨自辰,杨大成,1991.科技英语写作[M].北京:国防工业出版.
张春柏,王大伟,2017.英语笔译实务(三级)[M].北京:外文出版社.
张培基,2018.英汉翻译教程[M].修订本.上海:上海外语教育出版社.
NEWMARK P A,1988. A textbook of translation[M]. New York:Prentice Hall.
BAKER M,1992. In other words:a coursebook on translation[M]. London:Routledge.